I0110410

Sticky Feet

DIRECTIONS IN DEVELOPMENT
Trade

Sticky Feet

*How Labor Market Frictions Shape the Impact
of International Trade on Jobs and Wages*

Claire H. Hollweg, Daniel Lederman, Diego Rojas,
and Elizabeth Ruppert Bulmer

THE WORLD BANK
Washington, D.C.

© 2014 International Bank for Reconstruction and Development / The World Bank
1818 H Street NW, Washington DC 20433
Telephone: 202-473-1000; Internet: www.worldbank.org

Some rights reserved

1 2 3 4 17 16 15 14

This work is a product of the staff of The World Bank with external contributions. The findings, interpretations, and conclusions expressed in this work do not necessarily reflect the views of The World Bank, its Board of Executive Directors, or the governments they represent. The World Bank does not guarantee the accuracy of the data included in this work. The boundaries, colors, denominations, and other information shown on any map in this work do not imply any judgment on the part of The World Bank concerning the legal status of any territory or the endorsement or acceptance of such boundaries.

Nothing herein shall constitute or be considered to be a limitation upon or waiver of the privileges and immunities of The World Bank, all of which are specifically reserved.

Rights and Permissions

This work is available under the Creative Commons Attribution 3.0 IGO license (CC BY 3.0 IGO) http://creativecommons.org/licenses/by/3.0/igo. Under the Creative Commons Attribution license, you are free to copy, distribute, transmit, and adapt this work, including for commercial purposes, under the following conditions:

Attribution—Please cite the work as follows: Hollweg, Claire H., Daniel Lederman, Diego Rojas, and Elizabeth Ruppert Bulmer. 2014. *Sticky Feet: How Labor Market Frictions Shape the Impact of International Trade on Jobs and Wages.* Directions in Development. Washington, DC: World Bank. doi:10.1596/978-1-4648-0263-8. License: Creative Commons Attribution CC BY 3.0 IGO

Translations—If you create a translation of this work, please add the following disclaimer along with the attribution: *This translation was not created by The World Bank and should not be considered an official World Bank translation. The World Bank shall not be liable for any content or error in this translation.*

Adaptations—If you create an adaptation of this work, please add the following disclaimer along with the attribution: *This is an adaptation of an original work by The World Bank. Responsibility for the views and opinions expressed in the adaptation rests solely with the author or authors of the adaptation and are not endorsed by The World Bank.*

Third-party content—The World Bank does not necessarily own each component of the content contained within the work. The World Bank therefore does not warrant that the use of any third-party-owned individual component or part contained in the work will not infringe on the rights of those third parties. The risk of claims resulting from such infringement rests solely with you. If you wish to re-use a component of the work, it is your responsibility to determine whether permission is needed for that re-use and to obtain permission from the copyright owner. Examples of components can include, but are not limited to, tables, figures, or images.

All queries on rights and licenses should be addressed to the Publishing and Knowledge Division, The World Bank, 1818 H Street NW, Washington, DC 20433, USA; fax: 202-522-2625; e-mail: pubrights@worldbank.org.

ISBN (paper): 978-1-4648-0263-8
ISBN (electronic): 978-1-4648-0264-5
DOI: 10.1596/978-1-4648-0263-8

Cover art: © N.I / Dreamstime.com. Used with permission. Further permission required for reuse.

Cover design: Debra Naylor, Naylor Design

Library of Congress Cataloging-in-Publication Data has been requested.

Contents

Box

Figures

Map

Tables

Acknowledgments

Design of the analytical framework for estimating labor mobility and adjustment costs and the research reflected in this report were undertaken and supported by the International Trade Department of the Poverty Reduction and Economic Management (PREM) network of the World Bank. The team was led by Daniel Lederman (World Bank) and comprised Claire H. Hollweg (World Bank), Diego Rojas (World Bank), Elizabeth Ruppert Bulmer (World Bank), Francisco Javier Arias-Vázquez (World Bank), Erhan Artuç (World Bank), Germán Bet (Northwestern University), Irene Brambilla (Universidad Nacional de la Plata, Argentina), David Kaplan (Inter-American Development Bank), Gladys López-Acevedo (World Bank), Devashish Mitra (Syracuse University), Guido Porto (Universidad Nacional de la Plata, Argentina), Raymond Robertson (Macalester College), Yevgeniya Savchenko (World Bank), and Julia Oliver (World Bank). The team gratefully acknowledges the support and guidance of Mona Haddad (sector manager, International Trade Department, PREM network, World Bank), Jeffrey Lewis (director, PREM network, World Bank), and peer reviewers William Maloney (World Bank), David Newhouse (World Bank), and Samuel Freije-Rodríguez (World Bank). They also gratefully acknowledge insights from conversations with Mourad Bentahar, John McLaren, Stefano Paternostro, Abdoulaye Sy, Mohammed Taamouti, Paolo Verme, Anabel González, Francisco Monge, David Sequeira, and Michael Ferrantino.

The following background papers were commissioned for this analysis:

- F. J. Arias-Vázquez, E. Artuç, D. Lederman, and D. Rojas: "Trade, Informal Employment, and Labor Adjustment Costs"
- F. J. Arias-Vázquez and D. Lederman: "Displaced Workers and Labor Market Outcomes: Evidence from Mexico"
- E. Artuç, G. Bet, I. Brambilla, and G. Porto: "A Mapping of Labor Mobility Costs in the Developing World"
- C. H. Hollweg, D. Lederman, and D. Mitra: "Structural Reforms and Labor-Market Outcomes: International Panel Data Evidence"
- D. Kaplan, D. Lederman, and R. Robertson: "Worker-Level Adjustment Costs in a Developing Country: Evidence from Mexico"
- G. López-Acevedo and Y. Savchenko: "Trade Adjustment Assistance Programs"

About the Authors

Claire H. Hollweg is a consultant at the International Trade Department of the World Bank. She holds a PhD and an MA in economics from the University of Adelaide. Prior to studying economics, she worked as a journalist in newspaper and radio. She also has work experience with the government of South Australia and the Pacific Economic Cooperation Council (PECC) in Singapore. Her research interests include development economics with a recent focus on trade and labor and household responses to shocks.

Daniel Lederman is the lead economist and deputy chief economist for the Latin America and the Caribbean region in the World Bank, and previously served as lead trade economist in the World Bank's International Trade Department. He has published numerous books and articles on issues related to economic development, including financial crises, crime, political economy, growth, international trade, and labor markets. His research has been published in the *American Economic Review, Journal of Law and Economics, Journal of Development Economics,* and the *Journal of International Business Studies,* among others. He holds a PhD from the Johns Hopkins University School of Advanced International Studies.

Diego Rojas is a consultant in the Office of the Chief Economist for the Latin America and the Caribbean region in the World Bank. Before joining the World Bank, he worked as a lecturer and full-time researcher at the University of Costa Rica, where he obtained his MSc degree in economics. Between 2009 and 2013 he was a consultant for the Development Research Group and the International Trade Department of the World Bank. His most recent work has focused on labor markets and international trade.

Elizabeth Ruppert Bulmer is a senior economist at the World Bank, with extensive operational and research experience in Latin America and the Caribbean and in the Middle East and North Africa. Her research interests span labor issues and their links with trade and growth, and she is currently leading the research agenda on the labor market implications of trade in the World Bank's International Trade Department. She has published in the *Journal of Development Economics* and the *World Bank Economic Review,* and holds a PhD in economics from the University of Maryland.

Abbreviations

ALMP	active labor market policy
CAP	Common Agricultural Policy, EU
EIA	*Encuesta Industrial Anual* (Annual Industrial Survey), Argentina
ENOE	*Encuesta Nacional de Ocupación y Empleo* (National Occupation and Employment Survey), Mexico
EPH	*Encuesta Permanente de Hogares* (Permanent Household Survey), Argentina
EU	European Union
GMM	Generalized Method of Moments
IFS	*International Financial Statistics*
ILO	International Labour Organization
IMSS	*Instituto Mexicano del Seguro Social* (Mexican Social Security Institute)
OLS	ordinary least squares
OJT	on-the-job training
PLMP	passive labor market policy
PPP	purchasing power parity
TAA	Trade Adjustment Assistance
TED	*Total Economy Database*
UNIDO	United Nations Industrial Development Organization
WDI	*World Development Indicators*

Executive Summary

Linking Trade Reforms and Labor Outcomes

After two decades of global trade liberalization and other structural reforms, most developing countries today are open and well integrated into the global economy. Openness helps diversify sources of economic fluctuations, which is good for economic stability. It mitigates the impact of changes in domestic demand and supply on domestic prices, for example, and gives countries new opportunities for growth by expanding their access to international markets.[1]

But the new openness also has destabilizing effects: it broadens the exposure of developing countries to external shocks and increased competition from foreign markets. And because many developing countries are now liberalizing sectors of their economies, workers and firms in those sectors bear the brunt of the shocks. Increased prices for inputs used to create finished products, for instance, or fluctuations in external demand may translate into such disruptions as layoffs or factory closings. As governments pursue deeper reforms, they often face opposition from segments of the population concerned about how liberalization will affect local jobs and wages.

Understanding this tension between trade openness and employment is increasingly important to development. As trade liberalization has continued apace, its impact on job creation is attracting increasing attention. Moreover, the shape of the trade policies a country ultimately adopts will be influenced by the expected impact on workers, underlining the centrality of jobs to the trade policy agenda. The World Bank recently spotlighted the importance of jobs, asserting in its 2013 *World Development Report* that "jobs are the cornerstone of economic and social development" and that "jobs are transformational—they can transform what we earn, what we do, and even who we are" (World Bank 2012, 2).

To better understand this tension, the transmission channels from trade policies to labor markets, and the magnitude of their impact, this report analyzes how labor markets in developing countries adjust to permanent trade-related shocks. Examples of such shocks are changes in trade policy, whether at home or abroad, and enduring changes in international trade patterns that affect prices in global markets. These are distinguished from transitory shocks and other short-run business-cycle fluctuations in that the shocks that result from economy-wide reallocations of labor are not temporary but permanent. Trade-related shocks affect the relative prices faced by domestic firms and thus the relative demand for labor across industries. For example, a shock that expands trade would increase demand for labor in export-expanding sectors and reduce demand in import-competing ones.

Confronted with a new incentive framework caused by a permanent trade shock, workers in contracting sectors may decide to move to export-expanding sectors or they may be forced to find alternative employment due to lay-offs. If domestic labor markets were frictionless, workers would instantly benefit from international integration by being reallocated to the most productive activities. In reality, however, workers cannot move without cost. For instance, they may face periods of unemployment, job search, and/or retraining in order to change jobs and may have to relocate to a geographically distant location.

Two Cost Metrics: Labor Mobility and Labor Adjustment

The analysis distinguishes between two key labor market concepts: labor mobility costs and labor adjustment costs. *Labor mobility costs* are costs perceived by a worker to move to a different firm or industry independent of the reason for the move. When, however, workers are unable to move in response to an exogenous shock, such as a change in trade policy or in the international market, the total costs *incurred* by workers (and the economy) are defined as *labor adjustment costs*. In effect, adjustment costs due to sluggish reallocation of labor in response to a trade-related shock exist because of mobility costs.

To illustrate the distinction, when trade liberalization reduces the relative price of the output of a factory and that factory downsizes, laid-off workers face costs in moving to new jobs, costs that may be sustained over time. The magnitude of these labor adjustment costs depends on the size of the static mobility costs each worker would face in voluntarily making a shift, even if the factory had not downsized. When these costs are significant, workers may exhibit "sticky feet" by choosing to remain in their current sector or delay their transition rather than incur the costs of moving to better employment. Labor market frictions therefore shape the impact of international integration on employment outcomes by affecting how quickly workers transition to new jobs, and how wages adjust as a result. In this sense, labor adjustment costs reflect the difference between optimal worker welfare when labor mobility costs are zero and actual worker welfare when labor mobility costs are non-zero.

Well-functioning labor markets are vital to development, and labor adjustment costs matter a great deal in the context of trade liberalization. They can sometimes be so large that they more than offset the welfare improvements from tariff reductions that lower domestic prices and raise real wages. If labor reallocations across industries and employers are costly, the gains from trade might be reduced or even completely eliminated (Davidson and Matusz 2010). This phenomenon has political consequences: if not for the adjustment costs, globalization would be universally supported by workers in labor-abundant developing economies. To the extent that adjustment costs impede labor reallocations, they lead to idle workers or workers stuck in lower productivity firms and industries. This in turn implies lost incomes and diminished GDP gains from trade (Menezes-Filho and Muendler 2011, McCaig and Pavnick 2012, Bolaky and Freund 2004).

Analytical Tools

This report analyzes the adjustment costs of the labor reallocations that follow shocks, the ways in which mobility costs affect workers' employment decisions and thus labor market outcomes, and some of the mechanics of how those costs are distributed across workers and firms. But to measure labor adjustment costs, it is first necessary to measure labor mobility costs. This requires reliance on indirect measures because the various components of worker-specific mobility costs are not observable.

The research team and the World Bank Poverty Reduction and Economic Management International Trade department (PRMTR) have developed methodological approaches to estimate various aspects of the labor market impact of trade shocks when there are labor market frictions. These analytical tools take into account the types of data available for developing countries. The first approach estimates labor mobility and adjustment costs at both the aggregate level for a large sample of countries and a more detailed level using a small subset of developing countries. Underpinning these analyses is a structural model of workers' choice of employment sector, which is estimated using country-specific employment and wage data to derive the labor mobility costs that are used to generate adjustment cost estimates. The second approach, which uses empirical regression techniques as a robustness check, examines the impact of structural reforms and job displacement on labor market outcomes.

The analytical framework presented here is designed to help policymakers address a range of policy questions related to the labor effects of trade shocks, such as

- How do employment and wages respond to a sector-specific trade reform?
- What are the employment and wage responses in other sectors?
- For which sectors are worker entry costs highest?
- How do mobility costs vary for informal and formal sector workers?
- How long does it take for wages to recover to pre-shock levels?

The methodologies utilized in this report are adapted to different types of data and different levels of data aggregation. Sources range from sector-level data on employment and average wages for multiple years from, e.g., the UNIDO Industrial Statistics Database; panel data on individual worker's sector of employment and wages from household surveys, labor force surveys or administrative records (e.g., social security records); and panel firm-level survey data on output, investment, and labor.

For many developing countries, limited data mean that estimates of labor mobility costs and their correlates are possible only at the aggregated country level, but where more detailed data are available, the analysis uses more sophisticated tools. For countries with panel datasets of individual workers' sector of employment and the sector's average wage spanning multiple years, the team has created a Trade and Labor Adjustment Costs Toolkit. This toolkit, described in chapter 3 and applied in chapter 4 to Mexico, Brazil, and Morocco, can be used to estimate the labor effects of trade shocks on labor market outcomes disaggregated, for example, by sector, formality status, and firm size, which makes for a very rich analysis.

Main Findings

The findings of the analysis begin to address a major gap in the literature, which has to date provided little evidence about the trade-related adjustment costs of workers in developing countries and how adjustment costs are affected by worker mobility costs. The findings could be helpful to policymakers hoping to mitigate negative short-term consequences of trade liberalization and facilitate labor adjustment so as to accelerate the transition to a competitive, trade-supportive labor market.

The presence of labor market frictions reduces the potential gains from trade reform. When tariffs are reduced in one sector, the resulting change in relative prices raises real wages in some sectors and reduces real wages in the liberalized sector. The wage gaps that emerge lead to labor reallocation. But workers typically incur costs to change jobs; the magnitude of the mobility costs affects a worker's decisions about seeking alternative employment in a new firm, sector, or region. The higher the mobility costs, the slower the transition to the new steady state in the labor market. Workers' sticky feet result in forgone welfare gains from trade in terms of employment and earnings.

Workers, rather than firms, bear the brunt of adjustment costs. When a trade shock hits a developing country, the costs associated with worker decisions are notably higher than those associated with employer decisions. That is, the labor mobility costs borne by workers far outweigh labor adjustment costs borne by firms. A firm's adjustment cost might be lost profits because of an overextended payroll or a short-term inability to sell unneeded capital assets, for example. But the costs incurred by workers in terms of lost or reduced wages or spells of unemployment far outweigh firm costs. These findings are illustrated by the case of Argentina, where simulation of a large, positive trade shock is shown to benefit firm profits proportionally more than worker wages.

Mobility costs are much higher for workers in developing countries than for those in developed countries. Not only are workers in any country worse off than firms when a negative trade shock hits, but workers in developing countries are more vulnerable than those in developed countries. This report for the first time provides evidence that mobility costs for workers in developing economies are very high, averaging 4.93 times the annual wage and more than twice as high as costs for workers in developed economies.

Mobility costs vary by sector of employment. There is significant heterogeneity in the mobility costs for workers entering different industries, costs that may be positively related to the amount of "specific" rather than "general" skills needed in that industry. In Mexico, the industries with the lowest entry costs for formal workers are construction, services, and retail and wholesale trade; transportation and communications and utilities have the highest costs of entry. These findings could help policymakers to identify industries that are more difficult for workers to access, pointing to potential underlying factors, and highlighting the importance of considering labor mobility costs at the industry rather than the aggregate level.

The cost to enter formal employment is significantly higher than the cost to enter informal employment. The report reveals important details about how labor markets respond to shocks. A worker changing employment faces two potential sources of mobility friction: moving from one industry to another industry, and moving between informal and formal employment. Labor markets in Morocco, Mexico, and Brazil demonstrate that if a worker is transitioning from informal to formal employment, it is always less costly to stay in the same industry—costs are higher if the formal work is in a different industry. The lowest mobility costs are incurred in switching from formal to informal employment. In fact, trade liberalization that reduces domestic prices and increases real wages can increase the share of informal employment. But this is not because laid-off factory workers are transitioning to work in the informal sector, such as street-vending or informal childcare. Rather, trade reforms in developing countries increase average real wages, incentivizing workers to enter the labor force, thereby increasing economy-wide employment. Workers often choose to enter the labor force through the informal sector because it is easier. This is clearly illustrated in simulations using data from Morocco, Mexico, and Brazil: although informal employment increased after a simulated tariff reduction, formal employment remained fairly constant.

Certain sectors, which differ by country, provide an easier path to formal employment. In Mexico and Morocco, manufacturing appears to be a stepping stone into formal jobs because the cost of switching from informal to formal jobs is low. This is also true of the hospitality sector (restaurants and hotels) in Morocco and commerce in urban Brazil.

Labor adjustment costs can be very large. Lost earnings are the main preoccupation of trade reform. While it is generally understood that in the long run, liberalization of trade will lead to higher wages and employment, in the short run workers in some sectors may suffer. This leads to the fundamental question about worker welfare: How long will it take for a displaced worker to return to her previous wage level? The simulated dynamic adjustment paths of sectoral wages and employment following a trade shock indicate periods ranging by country from 2 to 15 years, with a new steady state typically reached within 10 years.

For workers in the liberalized food and beverages sector, for example, the gains tend to be positive and large: despite an initial decline in real wages, it is usually temporary and wages fully recover over time. The simultaneous increase in real wages in other sectors draws new entrants—including food and beverage as well as inactive workers—thus increasing employment in other sectors. The findings of this study support previous studies showing that liberalization leads to higher aggregate employment and higher wages.

Some labor market dynamics are country-specific. Firm size appears to affect labor mobility costs in some countries; in Morocco, for example, it is easier for a worker to find employment in a large firm (more than 100 employees) than a small firm (30 employees or fewer). The analysis estimates average labor mobility costs in 11 separate industries, which allows policymakers to differentiate effects by sector and better target policies following a trade-related shock. For example, the relative increase in employment in larger firms after a permanent trade shock outweighs that in smaller firms.

Workers displaced by plant closings suffer longer than other separated workers. Analysis of worker transitions in Mexico shows that for workers displaced by a plant closing, unemployment is longer and wage recovery slower than for those who quit, were fired, or closed their own businesses. It takes an estimated nine years for a worker displaced by a plant closing to recover her wages, three years for a worker who voluntarily quits, and four years for those who close their own businesses. Displacement due to plant closure does not preclude the possibility of future formal employment, however; within a year of the closing, both displaced and other separated workers face an equal probability of employment in the formal sector.

Policy Implications

The need for public labor adjustment assistance programs rises with the total cost of adjustment. Since individual workers cannot anticipate trade shocks, the costs of adjustment cannot be fully internalized beforehand. If workers could change jobs without cost within and across industries, there would be no need for public intervention. And because capital markets are imperfect, particularly in developing countries, workers are unlikely to be able to find financing to cover inter-industry mobility costs. At the other extreme, however, if interventions are overly generous, the process of adjustment may be thwarted. Labor adjustment programs should therefore be carefully designed or the benefits of existing social protection programs enhanced to reduce mobility costs and facilitate labor adjustment. Moreover, labor adjustment programs used as compensation schemes could mobilize political support for trade reforms.

Some major policy implications emerge from the report's analysis. Because workers bear the brunt of labor adjustment costs, it is important that policy solutions be aimed primarily at reducing labor mobility costs rather than firm-side labor adjustment costs. Policy design should therefore focus on minimizing worker mobility costs and accelerating their employment transitions.

Governments might consider putting in place programs that alleviate labor adjustment costs but do not prevent the economy-wide restructuring that accompanies trade liberalization. These policies would be second-best to programs that facilitate mobility if they effectively act as disincentives to moving.

The Trade and Labor Adjustment Costs Toolkit can be used to test for the potential sector-level effects of prospective changes in trade policy. If trade liberalization is likely to lead to plant closures, for example, policymakers should be aware that for laid-off workers wage recovery is relatively slower. Traditional social safety nets that provide temporary relief might not be sufficient because trade shocks tend to have more permanent effects. Toolkit estimates of the size of forgone gains to trade could be used to convince policymakers of the rationale for government intervention through labor adjustment assistance programs, but it is not the right instrument for designing specific policy parameters. This report describes a range of labor adjustment policies, lessons from specific countries, and pros and cons associated with each, leading to the following general lessons for informing policy design:

- *Context-specific*: Concentrating on specific sectors or using only specific instruments could be more effective than spreading resources thinly across numerous labor adjustment assistance programs. Therefore, to be effective, assistance programs in developing countries should be context-specific. Providing comprehensive programs that incorporate different support instruments would be too costly.

- *Minimize distortions*: Careful analysis is needed of ways to minimize distortions that might be created by adjustment programs, such as wage distortions.

- *Cost-sharing*: A variety of cost-sharing options for labor adjustment policies should be considered. For instance, the Austrian Steel Foundation is financed by a range of participating parties: trainees, firms, local governments, and other workers in the industry.

- *Design of retraining*: Given their generally poor track record, it is important to design any retraining programs carefully; training programs tend to be expensive but provide only small improvements in employment and virtually no improvements in the earnings of program participants compared to nonparticipant displaced workers. Cost-sharing of training programs by workers could help address the incentive issue.

- *Wage insurance or subsidies*: Theoretical models predict that wage subsidies for workers that move from shrinking to expanding sectors could be an efficient way to compensate losers at the lowest cost. Impact evaluations find that wage subsidies increase the probability of employment for program participants. Moreover, on-the-job training (OJT) tends to be more effective than other training, and wage subsidies could accelerate access to OJT.

Note

1. On the growth effects of trade, see Sachs and Warner (1995), Frankel and Romer (1999), Wacziarg and Welch (2008), Feyrer (2009), Arkolakis, Costinot, and Rodriguez-Clare (2012), Brückner and Lederman (2012), among others.

References

Arkolakis, C., A. Costinot, and A. Rodriguez-Clare. 2012. "New Trade Models, Same Old Gains?" *American Economic Review* 102 (1): 94–130.

Bolaky, B., and C. Freund. 2004. "Trade, Regulations, and Growth." Policy Research Working Paper 3255, World Bank, Washington, DC.

Brückner, M., and D. Lederman. 2012. "Trade Causes Growth in Sub-Saharan Africa." Policy Research Working Paper 6007, World Bank, Washington, DC.

Davidson, C., and S. J. Matusz. 2010. *International Trade with Equilibrium Unemployment.* Princeton, NJ: Princeton University Press.

Feyrer, J. 2009. "Trade and Income—Exploiting Time Series in Geography." NBER Working Paper 14910, National Bureau of Economic Research, Cambridge, MA.

Frankel, J., and D. Romer. 1999. "Does Trade Cause Growth?" *American Economic Review* 89 (3): 379–99.

Menezes-Filho, N. A., and M.-A. Muendler. 2011. "Labor Reallocation in Response to Trade Reform." NBER Working Paper 17372, National Bureau of Economic Research, Cambridge, MA.

McCaig, B., and N. Pavnick. 2012. "Export Markets and Labor Allocation in a Poor Country." Unpublished manuscript, Dartmouth College.

Sachs, J., and A. Warner. 1995. "Economic Reforms and the Process of Global Integration." *Brookings Papers on Economic Activity* 1: 1–118.

Wacziarg, R., and K. H. Welch. 2008. "Trade Liberalization and Growth: New Evidence." *World Bank Economic Review* 22 (2): 187–231.

World Bank. 2012. *Jobs: World Development Report 2013.* Washington, DC: International Bank for Reconstruction and Development/World Bank.

CHAPTER 1

Introduction

Overview

This report analyzes the paths by which developing country labor markets adjust to permanent trade-related shocks. Such shocks include changes in trade policy at home or abroad as well as medium-term changes in international trade patterns. They are distinct from transitory shocks, such as the global financial crisis of 2008–09 and other short-run fluctuations in the business cycle. Temporary shocks may require mitigation rather than adjustment; permanent shocks result in economy-wide reallocations of labor. The transmission channel from trade policy to labor markets is through relative prices: changes in global markets or countries' trade policies affect the relative prices confronting domestic firms and thus relative demand for labor across industries. For example, a shock that expands trade, such as a tariff reduction, would raise demand for labor in export-expanding sectors and reduce demand in import-competing sectors.

The speed with which labor markets—and employment and wages—respond to economic shocks depends on the ease of labor mobility. If domestic labor markets were frictionless and adjustments occurred instantaneously, workers would immediately benefit from international integration through higher average wages and expanded employment opportunities. Domestic factors of production—labor, capital, land—would always be allocated to the most productive activities, and workers would move seamlessly between farms and factories. In reality, however, workers cannot make such adjustments without cost. They face periods of job search, may need retraining, and for new employment may also need to relocate their residence to a geographically distant location. Family ties may also increase the cost of moving, as would the resulting decline in social capital as old networks are disrupted and new networks take time to establish. Such distortions create "sticky feet" that prevent or delay workers from moving to new industries in search of better employment opportunities.

These labor market frictions associated with worker mobility in turn shape how international integration affects employment outcomes. Understanding the aggregate costs of labor reallocations due to trade-related shocks (labor *adjust-ment* costs) first requires an understanding of the nature and magnitude of costs incurred by workers to move to alternative employment (labor *mobility* costs). Mobility costs refer to the perceived cost for a worker to move to a new industry or firm under normal circumstances (in steady state); adjustment costs refer to the total costs that arise due to sluggish labor reallocation in response to exogenous changes in prices. Assessing the dynamic adjustment path of labor markets to permanent trade-related shocks and calculating its costs first involves estimating labor mobility costs.

Labor Mobility and Labor Adjustment Costs Defined

Understanding labor mobility is essential to understanding how a labor market responds to trade shocks. In this report, labor mobility refers to the ability of workers to move between firms and industries in search of alternative employment opportunities, for example, in response to wage differences. Workers are often unable to make instant and effortless transitions because moving involves costs. *Labor mobility costs measure what a worker perceives to be the cost of switching jobs.* Estimating them requires an understanding of the factors that keep workers in place even when there might be better opportunities in a different type of firm or a different industry.

Labor mobility costs can exist whenever friction in the labor market makes reallocations between firms or industries costly. Typical impediments are skill mismatches (wages forgone because of lower productivity); limitations to geographic mobility (relocating across distances); and severance and hiring costs (including those imposed by law or convention). Other factors may be location preferences, job search costs, and even the psychological costs of changing jobs. These impediments matter for economy-wide responses to increased international integration.

- *Skill mismatches.* Skills acquired in one industry may not be perfectly transferrable to another, or even to other firms within the same industry. In that case, a worker's productivity may not be the same in a different job, and workers that transition might be forced to accept lower wages. In fact, skill-specific education is found to reduce worker mobility and was one of the explanations of why unemployment in Poland was higher and more persistent than in Estonia as the European Union (EU) was enlarging (Lamo, Messina, and Wasmer 2010; for further analysis of this subject, see also Neal 1995 and Cooper and Haltiwanger 2006, among others).

- *Geography.* Distances between employment opportunities can also affect the magnitude of mobility costs, particularly when industries are spatially concentrated. For example, if manufacturing firms are located near ports but agricultural land is in the interior, then workers separated from manufacturing jobs might find it costly to migrate for opportunities in agriculture, and vice versa.

- *Policy distortions*. However well-intentioned labor market regulations to protect workers might be, such as severance pay rules, they raise the cost of separation or hiring. Firing and hiring costs are de facto taxes on mobility because they can impose implicit costs on moving between employers. This has been the focus of research on the growth effects of trade, and Bolaky and Freund (2004) have argued that the gains from trade diminish with labor-market distortions precisely because labor reallocations are thwarted by policy-mandated costs.

Trade shocks can bring about reallocation of labor between industries, but the presence of labor mobility costs implies economy-wide losses because they extend the period of economic adjustment. While *mobility* costs are the perceived worker-specific cost of moving between industries or firms, *adjustment* costs refer to the total costs that arise when workers are unable to move in response to a shock and the resulting labor reallocations across the economy are sluggish. With international integration, changes in global markets or a country's trade policies can affect the relative prices faced by domestic firms and the relative profitability of alternative economic activities. While this affects the relative demand of an industry for factors of production, such as capital and labor, factor levels will deviate from what would be optimal because firms and workers cannot freely and instantaneously adjust. Labor adjustment costs, which are reflected in the difference between optimal (without mobility costs) and actual worker welfare, are the economy-wide costs that are caused by the (trade-related) shock when labor mobility is costly. Labor mobility costs, by contrast, would exist without any adjustment-inducing shocks.

Labor adjustment costs may be borne by a range of agents: workers, firms, the government, and the economy. For example, the costs to workers may be reflected in lost wages and spells of unemployment; lost profits for firms due to an overextended payroll or depreciation due to unliquidated capital; or government fiscal costs associated with safety nets such as unemployment benefits. All imply economic gains forgone due to slow labor reallocation.

This report focuses primarily on the adjustment costs faced by workers after a trade shock, because of their magnitude and welfare implications and their policy relevance. The stylized facts emerging from the literature (see chapter 2) indicate that adjustment costs are borne disproportionately by workers rather than firms. From a policy viewpoint, understanding the relative magnitudes of labor mobility and adjustment costs can help policymakers design trade policies that are consistent with employment objectives, can be complemented by labor policies or support programs to facilitate labor transitions, or both. Moreover, because labor market outcomes differ by industry, firm, and type of worker, more targeted policy responses may be needed. Estimates of mobility and adjustment costs can be used by policymakers to target the workers and sectors most affected during transition periods following economic changes. Finally, workers displaced due to trade-related shocks may be affected differently than other types of separated workers. Traditional social safety nets designed to provide temporary relief might not be sufficient if trade shocks have more permanent effects; in that case there may be a role for targeted trade adjustment assistance (TAA) programs.

Measurement Challenges

The components of worker-specific labor mobility costs cannot be observed, which presents a measurement challenge. Because the cost components of mobility cannot be directly measured and aggregated to compute total costs, indirect measures must be used. The analysis for this report identifies mobility costs based on a structural model of workers' sectoral employment choice adapted from the literature. Different estimation methodologies can use either country-level data on sectoral employment and wages or micro-data on individual labor variables and how they have evolved over time. In brief, the mobility costs of workers depend on both their personal characteristics and preferences and on sector-specific characteristics. These costs in turn determine whether a worker looking at a wage gap chooses to remain or to change jobs. The methodology (box 1.1 and appendix A) therefore uses observed worker movements and wage gaps as a reflection of the expected costs of moving.

Not being directly observable, labor adjustment costs similarly require indirect measurement. As described in box 1.1 and detailed in appendix A, the derived estimates of labor mobility costs are used to infer the adjustment costs. First the dynamic paths of sectoral labor outcomes from a pre-shock steady state to a post-shock steady state are simulated when labor mobility is costly. These wage and employment outcomes are then compared to the potential or optimal outcomes when mobility costs are zero. The difference in worker welfare with and without mobility costs captures the forgone gains when mobility is costly, which are defined as labor adjustment costs.

This two-step methodology is used as the basis for a set of analytical tools to evaluate the size and impact of labor adjustment resulting from trade-related shocks when there are labor market frictions. The tools, designed relative to the types of data available for developing countries, are used to address a range of

---

Box 1.1 Estimating Labor Mobility and Adjustment Costs Using a Structural Choice Model

Labor mobility costs are estimated based on observed worker transitions between sectors in response to differences in wages. Using a structural model of workers' choice of sector, a worker employed in sector i chooses to remain employed there or to move to sector j based on incurring a cost (for simplicity it is assumed the economy has only two sectors). This cost has a fixed component, average mobility cost caused by labor market frictions, and a worker-specific component $\varepsilon^{i,j}$, the idiosyncratic cost of moving from sector i to sector j that captures personal circumstances, such as preferences or family constraints.

box continues next page

Box 1.1 Estimating Labor Mobility and Adjustment Costs Using a Structural Choice Model
(continued)

The worker's expected welfare in sector i, EV^i, is the present discounted value of her real wage, a sector-specific fixed nonpecuniary benefit, and an option value reflecting the possibility of moving to a different sector where wages are higher. If the wage in sector j rises, even if she never actually moves, a worker in sector i will experience an increase in welfare due to the higher option value. These components (wage, sector-specific nonpecuniary benefit, and option value) are specific to the sector, not the worker, but the idiosyncratic moving cost is specific to the worker.

In each period, the worker decides whether or not to move based on which sector offers higher expected welfare net of moving costs. The expected welfare benefit of moving from sector i to sector j, $(EV^j - EV^i)$, depends on the wage differential between the sectors. The worker will move from sector i to sector j if the expected welfare benefit of moving $(EV^j - EV^i)$ exceeds the cost of doing so $(C + \varepsilon^{i,j})$; that is, if:

$$EV^j - EV^i \geq C + \varepsilon^{i,j}.$$

Labor mobility costs can be estimated from the model using data on observed employment flows and wage differentials between sectors. The model of workers' choice of sector generates flows of workers across sectors of the economy and the solution to the model is the employment allocation. The flows of workers across sectors depend on the model's parameters inclusive of mobility costs C. It is then possible to estimate these parameters by matching the predicted flows of workers simulated by the model with the observed flows of workers in the data for each country. Estimation methodologies differ depending on the data available.

The resulting mobility cost estimates represent a key input variable for simulating the dynamic adjustment paths to the new equilibrium employment-wage outcomes in both the affected sector and other sectors of the economy after an exogenous trade-related shock. The resulting market-clearing employment and wage path solutions reflect workers' optimization of their utility dependent on expected wages and costs to change sectors.

Labor adjustment costs are estimated for each country facing a hypothetical trade-related sectoral shock and are calculated as the difference in workers' welfare between the *potential* post-shock equilibrium with zero labor mobility costs and the *actual* post-shock equilibrium with the costs.

The change in relative prices and real wages after the shock will induce some workers to reallocate their labor. The magnitude of this reallocation depends on the labor mobility costs. The new resulting equilibrium welfare of a worker, V, is compared to her initial pre-shock welfare, V_{pre}, and her potential maximum welfare, V_{max}, if mobility costs were zero. The maximum potential gains to trade (PG) are therefore $V_{max} - V_{pre}$, and the actual gains (G) are $V - V_{pre}$. Labor adjustment costs (LAC) representing the forgone welfare gains to trade due to labor mobility costs are therefore

$$LAC = PG - G = V_{max} - V.$$

Source: Artuç, Lederman, and Porto 2013.

policy questions. Table 1.1 describes each analytical tool, the data requirements, potential sources of data, and examples of policy questions each tool can be used to address.

Data limitations for many developing countries suggest that estimating labor mobility costs and their correlates is possible only at the country level, but more detailed data lend themselves to more sophisticated tools. For countries with panel datasets on individuals by sector of employment and wages spanning multiple years, this study uses several analytical approaches, including a new Trade and Labor Adjustment Costs Toolkit developed by the World Bank's International Trade Department to help policymakers evaluate the costs of the

Table 1.1 Analytical Tools for Estimating Labor Mobility and Adjustment Costs

Tool	Data required	Data sources	Policy questions
Estimating country-level labor mobility costs and their country-level correlates	Number of workers in each sector and average sector wage over time; aggregate country characteristics (e.g., GDP per capita, agriculture employment share, educational attainment)	UNIDO Industrial Statistics Database	How do labor mobility costs vary by country? Does the level of development or other factors correlate with labor mobility costs?
Trade and Labor Adjustment Costs Toolkit: Estimating labor mobility costs for entry into different sectors and by worker type	Panel time series data on individuals' sectoral employment, wages, and demographic characteristics	At least 2 household or labor force surveys with a panel component, or social security data for at least 2 years, or surveys with retrospective questions	Which sectors are more costly for workers to enter? What are the sectors that act as stepping stones out of agriculture? What sectors act as stepping-stones for informal employees to enter formal jobs? Is it harder for workers to enter large or small firms?
Trade and Labor Adjustment Costs Toolkit: Simulating dynamic employment and wage responses to a trade shock across economic sectors and worker types, and estimating the duration of the adjustment period and the labor adjustment costs	Estimates of labor mobility costs, labor share of sectoral production, and sectoral shares of total consumption	Estimates of labor mobility costs (see above), plus input-output tables	How much do workers in the liberalized sector gain? Do sectoral wages recover, and if so, how long does it take? What are the potential gains from trade without mobility costs? What are the forgone gains from trade due to mobility costs?
Estimating the relative cost of a trade shock to workers when firms face costly capital adjustment	Panel time series data on individuals' sectoral employment and wages; firm-level panel survey data on investment (purchases of new capital), sales of installed capital, employment and wages, and capital share in revenue	At least 2 household or labor force surveys with a panel component, or social security data for at least 2 years, and enterprise survey data with panel component	Do workers or firms gain more from a positive trade shock?

labor reallocations that follow shocks, how adjustment costs affect worker mobility decisions and thus labor market outcomes, and how those costs are distributed across workers and sectors.

To complement and validate the analysis based on structural choice models, the study designed a distinct empirical approach using reduced-form econometric estimation strategies. This approach examines the impact of structural reforms and worker displacement on labor market outcomes. This makes it possible to estimate the time required to adjust to a trade-related shock, but does not assume the rigid underlying relationship inherent in structural models. These reduced-form estimations act as a robustness check on the structural model estimates.

Scope of the Report

The rest of this report is organized as follows: Chapter 2 presents evidence from the literature on the relative magnitude of labor adjustment costs borne by workers and by firms. Chapter 3 presents a new database of country-level labor mobility cost estimates for both developing and developed economies. The estimates are then used to assess the correlates of country-level mobility costs and to simulate the impacts of trade-related shocks on labor market outcomes. The simulation results feed into estimates of labor adjustment costs, which can help policy analysts assess labor market responses to trade-related shocks by sector.

Chapter 4 showcases country case studies in which labor mobility costs vary by industry, firm size, and worker type (e.g., informal vs. formal). The analytical framework for these case studies is the basis for the Trade and Labor Adjustment Costs Toolkit, which estimates mobility and adjustment costs when panel data are available on workers' sector of employment and the sector's average wage. The toolkit identifies labor mobility costs using worker transitions between industries. These flows depend on the degree of aggregation of industry classification in the data; this can matter a great deal because the magnitudes of the estimates are sensitive to the number of industries chosen to be analyzed. This warrants a major caveat: cross-country estimates of labor mobility costs are only comparable when the same industry classification is used, as illustrated in chapter 3. The pilot case studies simulate the labor market dynamics of a trade-related shock. The analysis is extended by using firm-level data on capital investment, which allows for comparison of adjustment costs for workers when firms face costly capital adjustment.

Chapter 5 analyzes the impact of structural reforms on aggregate labor market outcomes across countries and the effect of worker displacement due to plant closings on the employment outcomes of individual workers in Mexico. In both cases, the empirical methodology, which relies on econometric regression estimations, is different from the structural models used in the previous chapters. The advantage of the results discussed in chapter 5 is that they give a sense of the time it takes for labor markets and individual workers to adjust to long-term trade-related shocks without imposing assumptions about how the underlying structural relationships operate. The results are nevertheless consistent with those from the structural estimations, which demonstrates the robustness of the Toolkit's analytical approach.

Chapter 6 concludes with a summary of the main findings about the labor adjustment costs associated with trade-related shocks and a discussion of policy responses internationally. It describes policy options for alleviating the costs of adjustment by reducing the frictions that create labor mobility costs, and second-best options centered on financial support to workers affected by permanent fluctuations in international trade. The gains from trade would be enhanced if policymakers can alleviate the costs of economy-wide adjustments.

References

Artuç, E., D. Lederman, and G. Porto. 2013. "A Mapping of Labor Mobility Costs in the Developing World." Policy Research Working Paper No. 6556, World Bank, Washington, DC.

Bolaky, B., and C. Freund. 2004. "Trade, Regulations, and Growth." Policy Research Working Paper 3255, World Bank, Washington, DC.

Cooper, R. W., and J. C. Haltiwanger. 2006. "On the Nature of Capital Adjustment Costs." *Review of Economic Studies* 73 (3): 611–33.

Lamo, A., J. Messina, and E. Wasmer. 2011. "Are Specific Skills an Obstacle to Labor Market Adjustment?" *Labour Economics* 18: 240–56.

Neal, D. 1995. "Industry-Specific Human Capital: Evidence from Displaced Workers." *Journal of Labor Economics* 13 (4): 653–77.

CHAPTER 2

Workers' Sticky Feet, Not Rusty Firms: Evidence from the Literature

Abstract

After reviewing stylized facts from previous studies of mobility and adjustment costs, this chapter concludes that the emphasis should no longer be on the distortions that affect firm costs of reallocating labor but rather on the distortions that affect worker mobility. It has been shown that most of the welfare impacts of shocks are borne by workers, not firms, because firms are more likely to respond to shocks by hiring or firing workers than by adjusting capital stocks. Firm-level adjustment costs for both capital and labor tend to be quite modest, especially in developing countries. Workers, on the other hand, have sticky feet. Because of the high costs of mobility they are much less flexible and consequently bear the brunt of adjustment costs.

The distinction between worker and firm adjustment costs is important when analyzing the welfare impacts of shocks. Labor adjustment costs are becoming a central component of models that analyze the effects of international integration on labor markets. Two strands of literature are concerned with estimation of adjustment costs. Although a series of studies has highlighted the importance of these costs to how economic agents respond to shocks, only recently have studies explicitly distinguished between labor adjustment costs on the demand (firm or employer) side and supply (worker) side of the market. Most of the welfare impacts of shocks have been found to fall on the supply side, suggesting that the adjustment costs borne by workers are much more important than those borne by firms.

Additional stylized facts documented in the literature are important to this report. Numerous studies of the demand side have directly estimated firm adjustment costs by looking at how quickly firm capital stocks and employment levels adjust to changes in fundamentals, such as exogenous productivity and price shocks. Often cited are Hamermesh (1993); Caballero, Engel, and Haltiwanger (1997); Cooper, Haltiwanger, and Power (1999); Caballero and Engle (1999); and Caballero et al. (2013). A few trade studies also use these models, for example, Utar (2008). More recent studies use estimates of labor mobility costs to simulate the costs of labor adjustment in response to changes in fundamentals; these have benefited greatly from the work of Artuç, Chaudhuri, and McLaren (2010), which is the approach taken in this analysis.[1]

Adjustments costs are a major obstacle to microeconomic flexibility. By most efficiently facilitating the prompt allocation of factors of production, flexibility is at the core of productivity and economic growth (Caballero, Engel, and Micco 2004). A flexible firm is one in which the gap between optimal and actual factor utilization levels is reduced quickly by rapid adjustments of capital and labor in response to a shock; for an inflexible firm the gap persists over time. Adjustment costs create rigidities, which can be costly for growth, especially in developing countries like Chile (Caballero, Engel, and Micco 2004).

Adjustment costs amplify the costs of aggregate shocks by causing firms to adjust capital and labor in a lumpy manner. Firms adjust by more when gaps between desired and actual levels are larger. Rather than small and frequent adjustments, when there are adjustment costs, the adjustments are large.[2] This result holds for adjustments to both capital and labor (Caballero, Engel, and Haltiwanger 1997) and in both developed and developing countries (Eslava et al. 2010).

The preponderance of evidence suggests that firms are more likely to respond to shocks by adjusting their workforce rather than their capital stock because adjusting labor costs less than adjusting capital (Eslava et al. 2010).[3] For example, evidence from the United States shows that large adjustments in flows in manufacturing employment can be attributed to aggregate shocks (Cabarrero, Engel, and Haltiwanger 1997). As figure 2.1 shows, employment responds disproportionately to aggregate shocks in the business cycle; for example, the two spikes in employment growth coincide with the first and second oil crises. This evidence that trade-related price shocks can lead to large adjustments in employment lends support to this report's focus on adjustment costs faced by workers, the supply side of the market.

Most studies support the finding that firm adjustment costs for both capital and labor tend to be quite modest, especially in developing countries.[4] Robertson and Dutkowsky (2002) found that in Mexico the labor adjustment costs of manufacturing firms are significantly lower than in the United States and the United Kingdom (see figure 2.2); labor adjustment costs in the aggregated manufacturing sector in the U.K. were 0.06 percent of the annual wage bill, whereas in manufacturing subsectors in Mexico, they ranged from less than 0.01 percent to 0.03 percent. Labor adjustment costs for manufacturing firms in the United States, although significantly higher, were nevertheless only 3 percent of the annual wage bill.

Firm adjustment costs for labor differ by type of firm as well as type of worker, suggesting other institutional factors may be at play. Even among developing countries in Latin America there are differences in demand-side costs. For example, Brazil, Colombia, and Chile demonstrate more microeconomic flexibility

Figure 2.1 Marginal Responses of Average Employment to Aggregate Shocks Are Significant

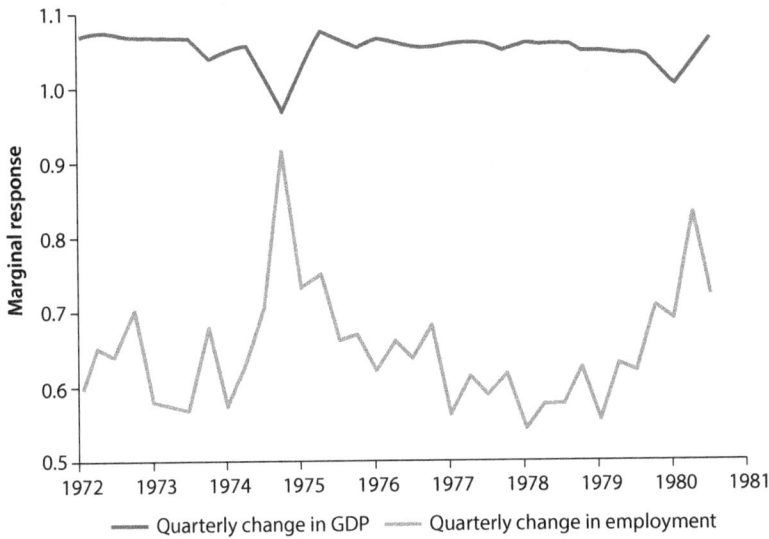

Source: Caballero, Engel, and Haltiwanger 1997.
Note: Figure 2.1 plots on the vertical axis the marginal response of average employment growth (orange/ lighter line) to aggregate shocks during the business cycle (blue/darker line, calculated as GDP fluctuations around its long-term trend) between quarters of 1972 and 1981 on the horizontal axis. The marginal response varies over time and is amplified by the effect of large shocks throughout the sample period.

Figure 2.2 Firm Labor Adjustment Costs Are Lower in Developing Countries

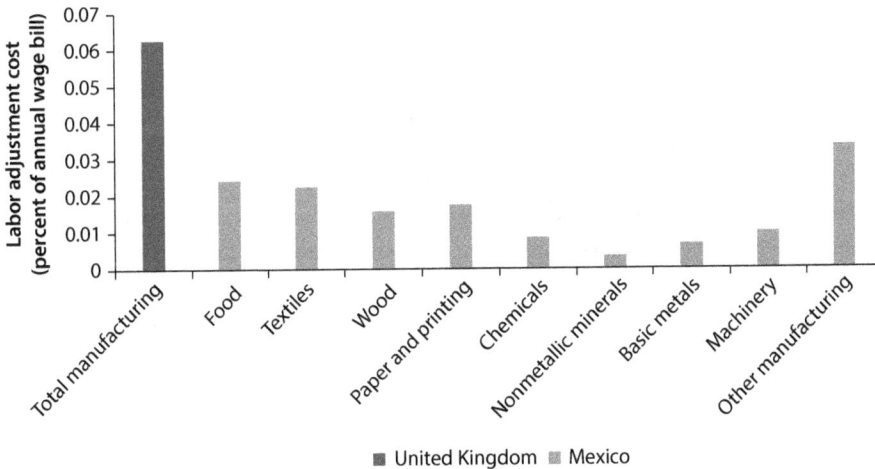

Sources: Burgess and Dolado 1989; Robertson and Dutkowsky 2002.

than Mexico. This result is mainly explained by differences in average firm size: small establishments are considerably less flexible than large ones that can adjust more promptly (Caballero, Engel, and Micco 2004). In addition to varying by industry and firm, firm labor adjustment costs also differ by worker type. Adjustment costs are higher for nonproduction than for production workers in

Mexico, with additional asymmetry related to training and unionization (Robertson and Dutkowsky 2002).[5] Casacuberta, Gandelman, and Olarreaga (2006) found larger adjustment costs for unskilled than for skilled manufacturing workers in Uruguay.

The conclusion that workers bear the brunt of adjustment costs to a shock because firms have lower adjustment costs for labor than for capital holds even in countries where regulation impedes the process of adjustment. Regulatory reforms affecting firms tend to have only modest implications for adjustment costs. This was the case in Colombia, for example (Eslava et al. 2010). Although it has been argued that eliminating regulations would yield substantial productivity gains by enhancing flexibility, the actual impact of the Colombian deregulation on aggregate productivity through factor adjustment was modest. This is not to say that regulations affecting firms do not matter. In fact, there is evidence that regulations matter for firm behavior and aggregate growth and productivity through firm entry and exit. Job security regulations have been found to interfere with the creative destruction process necessary for development, especially in countries where regulations are likely to be enforced—countries with strong rule of law (Caballero et al. 2013).

Comparing the flexibility of workers and firms, recent studies on labor mobility costs show that firms seem much more flexible, even in countries with onerous labor regulations. In the United States firm rigidities are negligible compared to worker rigidities, as shown by low adjustment costs for firms and high mobility costs for workers. For the United States Artuç, Chaudhuri, and McLaren (2010) found high average mobility costs for workers moving from one broadly aggregated sector of the economy to another—about 13 times average annual wages. Such high costs are in line with the related findings of Kennan and Walker (2003) and Artuç (2009). By contrast, Hamermesh (1993) estimated firm labor adjustment costs in the United States to be 4–5 percent of the wage bill.

When analyzing the labor market implications of trade shocks, the emphasis should therefore be on workers' sticky feet, not rusty firms. This calls for an increased focus on the distortions affecting worker mobility. Such distortions create sticky feet that prevent or delay workers from moving in search of better employment opportunities. The remainder of this report therefore focuses on the adjustment costs from trade-related shocks that workers themselves face.

Until now scholars have been relatively silent about the costs of adjustment for workers, especially in developing countries. The reason is that assessment of labor market responses and calculation of adjustment costs when labor mobility is imperfect requires data to estimate mobility costs that are seldom available for developing countries. One of the primary contributions of the research underpinning this report is the development of an analytical framework to estimate these costs for a large sample of developed and developing economies. Chapter 3 provides comparable estimates of mobility costs that are used to consider the impact of trade liberalization on labor market outcomes and to calculate the resulting adjustment costs.

Notes

1. Other contributions have come from Artuç, Chaudhuri, and McLaren (2008), Cosar (2013), Cosar, Gumer, and Tybout (2010), Davidson and Matusz (2006), Dix-Carneiro (2010), and Kambourov (2009). The labor literature has used similar models to estimate the impact of policy changes on labor adjustment, e.g., Lee (2005), Keane and Wolpin (1997), Kennan and Walker (2003), and Lee and Wolpin (2006).

2. This result has been documented throughout the literature, for example by Caballero, Engel, and Haltiwanger (1997), Cooper, Haltiwanger, and Power (1999), Caballero and Engle (1999), Caballero, Engel, and Micco (2004), Eslava et al. (2010), Doms and Dunne (1998), Gelos and Isgut (2001), Nilsen and Schiantarelli (2003), and Gourio and Kashyap (2007).

3. Of course, there will be some interaction between capital and labor adjustments when frictions in capital and labor adjustment reinforce each other. Firms facing capital shortages have been shown to reduce hiring and those facing labor surpluses to reduce capital shedding (Eslava et al. 2010). But most studies support the finding that firms have much more flexibility in adjusting labor than in adjusting capital.

4. See, for example, Hall (2004), Burgess and Dolado (1989), Shapiro (1986), Nickell (1986), Hamermesh (1989), Hamermesh and Pfann (1996), Robertson and Dutkowsky (2002).

5. Industries that require more training or that are more unionized tend to have higher labor adjustment costs as observed by lower labor adjustments (either in number of workers or hours of work).

References

Artuç, E. 2009. "Intergenerational Effects of Trade Liberalization," unpublished manuscript, International Trade Department, Poverty Reduction and Economic Management, World Bank, Washington, DC.

Artuç, E., S. Chaudhuri, and J. McLaren. 2008. "Delay and Dynamics in Labor Market Adjustment: Simulation Results." *Journal of International Economics* 75 (1): 1–13.

———. 2010. "Trade Shocks and Labor Adjustment: A Structural Empirical Approach." *American Economic Review* 100: 1008–45.

Burgess, S. M., and J. Dolado. 1989. "Intertemporal Rules with Variable Speed of Adjustment: An Application to U.K. Manufacturing Employment." *Economic Journal* 99: 347–65.

Caballero, R. J., K. N. Cowan, E. M. R. A. Engel, and A. Micco. 2013. "Effective Labor Regulation and Microeconomic Flexibility." *Journal of Development Economics* 101: 92–104.

Caballero, R. J., and E. M. R. A. Engel. 1999. "Explaining Investment Dynamics in U.S. Manufacturing: A Generalized (S,s) Approach." *Econometrica* 67 (4): 783–826.

Caballero, R. J., E. M. R. A. Engel, and J. Haltiwanger. 1997. "Aggregate Employment Dynamics: Building from Microeconomic Evidence." *American Economic Review* 87 (1): 115–37.

Caballero, R. J., E. M. R. A. Engel, and A. Micco. 2004. "Microeconomic Flexibility in Latin America." Center Discussion Paper 884, Economic Growth Center, Yale University, New Haven, CT.

Casacuberta, C., N. Gandelman, and M. Olarreaga. 2006. "Factor Adjustment and Imports from China and India: Evidence from Uruguayan Manufacturing." Unpublished manuscript.

Cooper, R. J., J. C. Haltiwanger, and L. Power. 1999. "Machine Replacement and the Business Cycle: Lumps and Bumps." *American Economic Review* 89: 921–46.

Cosar, A. K. 2013. "Adjusting to Trade Liberalization: Reallocation and Labor Market Polices." Working Paper, Booth School of Business, University of Chicago, Chicago, IL.

Cosar, A. K., N. Gumer, and J. Tybout. 2010. "Firm Dynamics, Job Turnover, and Wage Distributions in an Open Economy." NBER Working Paper 16326, National Bureau of Economic Research, Cambridge, MA.

Davidson, C., and S. J. Matusz. 2006. "Trade Liberalization and Compensation." *International Economic Review* 47 (3): 723–47.

Dix-Carneiro, R. 2010. "Trade Liberalization and Labor Market Dynamics." CEPS Working Paper 212, Center for Economic Policy Studies, Princeton University, Princeton, NJ.

Doms, M., and T. Dunne. 1998. "Capital Adjustment Patterns in U.S. Manufacturing Plants." *Review of Economic Dynamics* 1: 409–29.

Eslava, M., J. Haltiwanger, A. Kugler, and M. Kugler. 2010. "Factor Adjustments after Deregulation: Panel Evidence from Colombian Plants." *Review of Economics and Statistics* 92 (2): 378–91.

Gelos, R. G., and A. Isgut. 2001. "Fixed Capital Adjustment: Is Latin America Different?" *Review of Economics and Statistics* 83 (4): 717–30.

Gourio, F., and A. Kashyap. 2007. "Investment Spikes: New Facts and a General Equilibrium Explanation." *Journal of Monetary Economics* 54: 1–22.

Hall, R. E. 2004. "Measuring Factor Adjustment Costs." *Quarterly Journal of Economics* 119 (3): 899–927.

Hamermesh, D. S. 1989. "Labor Demand and the Structure of Adjustment Costs." *American Economic Review* 79 (4): 674–89.

———. 1993. *Labor Demand.* Princeton, NJ: Princeton University Press.

Hamermesh, D. S., and G. A. Pfann. 1996. "Adjustment Costs in Factor Demand." *Journal of Economic Literature* 34: 1264–92.

Kambourov, G. 2009. "Labour Market Regulations and the Sectoral Reallocation of Workers: The Case of Trade Reforms." *Review of Economic Studies* 76 (4): 1321–58.

Keane, M. P., and K. I. Wolpin. 1997. "The Career Decisions of Young Men." *Journal of Political Economy* 105 (3): 473–522.

Kennan, J., and J. R. Walker. 2003. "The Effect of Expected Income on Individual Migration Decisions." NBER Working Paper 9585, National Bureau of Economic Research, Cambridge, MA.

Lee, D. 2005. "An Estimable Dynamic General Equilibrium Model of Work, Schooling, and Occupational Choice." *International Economic Review* 46 (1): 1–34.

Lee, D., and K. I. Wolpin. 2006. "Intersectoral Labor Mobility and the Growth of the Service Sector." *Econometrica* 74 (1): 1–46.

Nickell, S. 1986. "Dynamic Models of Labor Demand." In *Handbook of Labor Economics,* Vol. I, edited by O. Ashenfelter and R. Layard, 473–522. Amsterdam: Elsevier.

Nilsen, O., and F. Schiantarelli. 2003. "Zeroes and Lumps in Investment: Empirical Evidence on Irreversibilities and Nonconvexities." *Review of Economics and Statistics* 85 (4): 1021–43.

Robertson, R., and D. H. Dutkowsky. 2002. "Labor Adjustment Costs in a Destination Country: The Case of Mexico." *Journal of Development Economics* 67: 29–54.

Shapiro, M. 1986. "The Dynamic Demand for Capital and Labor." *Quarterly Journal of Economics* 101: 513–42.

Utar, H. 2008. "Import Competition and Employment Dynamics." Unpublished manuscript, University of Colorado at Boulder.

CHAPTER 3

Mapping Labor Mobility and Labor Adjustment Costs around the World

Abstract

For workers considering a job change, moving costs are significant. These costs, which cannot be observed, vary by worker and sector. This chapter presents a sectoral choice model that makes it possible to estimate the costs using widely available data on sectoral employment and wages over time. The resulting estimates of labor mobility costs for 47 countries show how high the costs are, particularly in developing countries, and how they create frictions that impede labor adjustment after a trade shock. The chapter illustrates how a trade-related shock affects jobs and wages not only in the liberalized sector but also in the rest of the economy due to shifts in relative labor demand and supply. For the average worker starting off in the liberalized food and beverage sector, for example, actual gains from trade liberalization tend to be positive and large; the initial decline in real wages is usually temporary and wages fully recover over time. Moreover, the simultaneous increase in real wages in other sectors draws workers from the food and beverage sector, thereby increasing employment in other sectors. Nevertheless, mobility costs reduce the speed of transition to the new steady state and raise aggregate adjustment costs.

Labor Mobility Costs around the World

The mobility costs encountered by workers considering an employment change—whether to a new job in the same sector, to a new sector, or into unemployment—depend on worker, sector, and country characteristics. This chapter begins by exploring how average labor mobility costs compare across countries, and whether the costs are similar for workers in developing countries and those in developed countries.

As described in chapter 1, the analytical framework recognizes differences in mobility costs and measures them indirectly despite unobservable contributing factors. The structural choice methodology designed by Artuç, Lederman, and Porto (2013) for this report[1] identifies labor mobility costs using worker transitions across industries in response to differences in industry wages. As labor market frictions increase, workers become less responsive to differences in wages between industries; it can therefore be expected that when labor mobility costs are large, there would be larger wage differentials between sectors that have not seen large changes in labor allocations. But if mobility costs are small, workers would respond to even small wage differentials and, in equilibrium, inter-industry wage differentials would be smaller. The estimated labor mobility cost is interpreted as the average cost a worker would incur to move between industries for a given wage differential.

The framework is based on a structural model of workers' sectoral employment choices when labor mobility is costly. For simplicity, it is assumed that there are only two sectors in the economy, i and j. In each period, a worker employed in sector i decides whether to stay in sector i, for which she would receive an expected welfare of EV^i, or to move to sector j, but at a cost. The decision depends on the cost and the expected benefit of moving $(EV^j - EV^i)$, which in turn depends on the wage differential between the sectors. Because workers move for a variety of reasons that could be characterized as random (no single worker faces the same issues at the same time), the mobility cost incorporates a fixed component (the average mobility cost due to labor market frictions, C) and an idiosyncratic component (the worker-specific moving cost, $\varepsilon^{i,j}$). Examples of factors that contribute to the idiosyncratic component are family structure or life-changing decisions like marriage, or a birth or death in the family. The worker decides to move if the expected welfare of moving to sector j is greater than or equal to the expected welfare of staying in sector i plus the moving cost. That is, the worker decides to move if:

$$EV^j - EV^i \geq C + \varepsilon^{i,j}.[2]$$

For a given net benefit, as the mobility cost increases, the share of workers deciding to move declines. Conversely, for a given mobility cost, an increase in the net benefit will induce more workers to move. Figure 3.1 illustrates the relationship between the average moving cost C_1, the net benefit a worker expects to receive if she moves $(EV^j - EV^i$, measured on the horizontal axis), and the share of workers who move from sector i to sector j, S_{C_1} (measured on the vertical axis, equivalent to the probability of moving).[3] When the mobility cost increases from C_1 to C_2, for a given expected net benefit the share of workers deciding to move declines to S_{C_2}.

Labor reallocations will differ by country, and so too will the estimated mobility costs. Curves C_1 and C_2 in figure 3.1 could also represent two countries with different moving costs. In two otherwise identical economies, a country with more job switchers will have a lower estimated labor mobility cost of switching for given observed wage differentials.

From this framework is generated a database that maps average mobility costs per worker for 47 countries (see table 3.1). The mobility cost parameter, C, is estimated by matching the worker flows predicted by the model with real data on

Figure 3.1 A Graphic Representation of Labor Mobility Costs

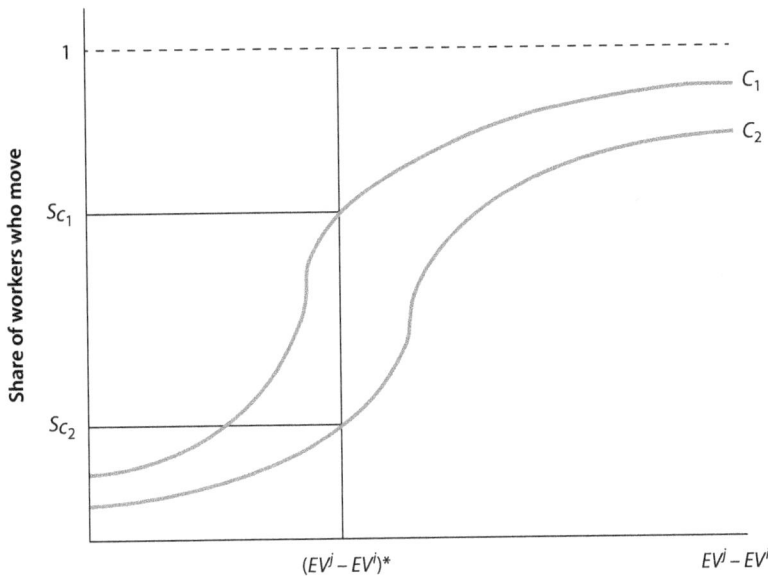

Note: The share of workers who move from sector *i* to sector *j* is measured on the vertical axis, and the net benefit they expect to receive by moving $(EV^j - EV^i)$ is measured on the horizontal axis. For a given mobility cost C, as the expected net benefit increases, more workers decide to move. It is assumed that C_2 is higher than C_1 $(C_2 > C_1)$. For a given level of net benefits $(EV^j - EV^i)^*$, the share of workers deciding to move, S_{C_1}, is higher when the cost is low (C_1) compared to the share, S_{C_2}, who decide to move when the cost is high (C_2).

observed average flows of workers and wages in each country.[4] Estimating labor mobility costs is data-intensive, which typically precludes multicountry analysis, especially for developing countries. One major contribution of this report is the development of a strategy that generates estimates of average labor mobility costs at the country level using limited data on net employment flows and average wages across industries.[5] It uses the UNIDO Industrial Statistics database for 1990–2008 for manufacturing data and national accounts data for nonmanufacturing employment shares, employing the same sectoral breakdown for all countries. Data are aggregated into nine sectors (see note to table 3.1). (Appendix A presents the model and estimation strategy more formally, and appendix B describes the data.)

The estimates of average labor mobility costs in table 3.1 indicate that

- *Labor mobility costs are high.* When switching sectors, the average worker faces a welfare cost equivalent to 3.75 times the annual average wage in the economy.
- *Mobility costs are higher for workers in developing countries than for those in developed countries.* On average, the mobility cost in developed countries is equivalent to 2.41 times the annual wage, less than half the average for developing countries, which is 4.93 times the annual wage.
- *Mobility costs vary significantly by country and region.* Estimated costs are highest in Peru, Azerbaijan, Turkey, Ethiopia, and Bangladesh and lowest in

Table 3.1 Average Labor Mobility Costs in Developing and Developed Countries
Ratio of the annual average wage

	Number of countries	Average labor mobility cost	Standard error
All countries	47	3.75	1.93
Developed	22	2.41	1.11
Developing	25	4.93	1.72
By region			
Western Europe	16	2.61	1.09
North America	2	1.65	0.69
Eastern Europe & Central Asia	8	4.96	2.21
South Asia	2	5.45	1.56
Latin America & Caribbean	5	5.34	1.93
East Asia & Pacific	5	3.03	2.34
Middle East & North Africa	5	4.40	0.37
Sub-Saharan Africa	4	4.26	2.12
By income			
High-income OECD	20	2.40	1.07
High-income non-OECD	2	2.55	2.06
Upper-middle-income	14	4.83	2.13
Lower-middle-income	9	4.68	0.69
Low-income	2	6.81	0.36

Source: Artuç, Lederman, and Porto 2013.
Note: Table 3.1 presents average labor mobility costs as a ratio of the annual average wage for various country groups, aggregated into nine sectors: metals and minerals; chemicals and petroleum products; machinery; food and beverages; wood products; textiles and clothing; miscellaneous equipment; motor vehicles; and a residual nonmanufacturing sector.

Singapore, followed by the United States and Japan. Costs are higher in South Asia and the Latin America and Caribbean region than in sub-Saharan Africa and the East Asia and Pacific region. Appendix C reports the results for each country, which are illustrated in map 3.1.

Correlates of Labor Mobility Costs

Labor mobility costs are correlated with aggregate indicators related to a country's well-being, labor market characteristics, educational attainment, and regulatory distortions. Figure 3.2 presents selected cross-country correlates of the costs (given by the estimates of C by country). Correlates are plotted on the vertical axis and estimates of average labor mobility costs on the horizontal axis for each country in the sample, and the curves are fitted from nonparametric regressions of the variables. The following conclusions emerge:

- *Richer countries tend to have lower mobility costs, but not because the adjustment costs of firms are lower.* While there is a weak correlation between mobility costs and firing costs, the correlation with GDP per capita is quite negative and robust. The upward-sloping section in the correlation with firing costs is small,

Map 3.1 Average Labor Mobility Costs
Ratio of the annual average wage

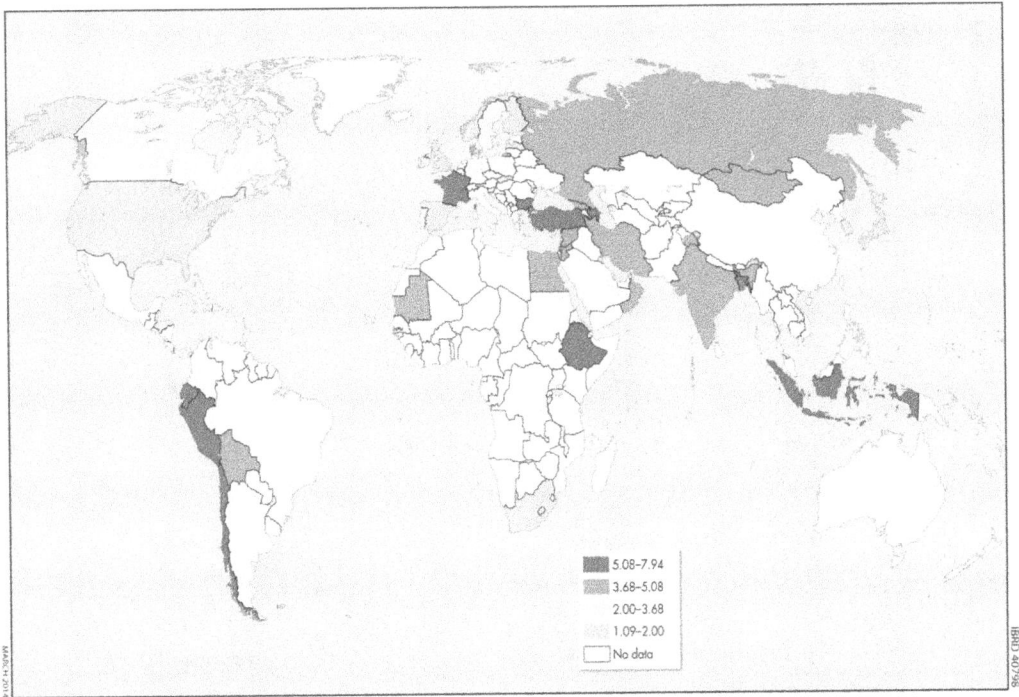

Source: Artuç, Lederman, and Porto 2013.

driven by a few outliers, and drops again. A linear regression would in fact be horizontal. These results are consistent with the assertion that distortions affecting firm labor adjustments (captured by firing costs) are not the main driver of mobility costs. There are also positive correlations with the poverty head-count and the poverty gap, but no obvious correlation with inequality.

- *Mobility costs tend to be lower in countries more highly specialized in nonprimary sectors or with highly educated workforces.* There is a positive correlation between mobility costs and employment shares in agriculture. The cost estimates are inversely correlated with tertiary educational attainment.[6] Also, countries with lower education quality (a higher pupil-teacher ratio) tend to have higher mobility costs.

- *Labor market rigidities are more prevalent in countries characterized by other types of rigidities and distortions.* Mobility costs are positively correlated with other frictions and constraints, such as time to export. But rather than border frictions causing mobility costs, a credible interpretation is that countries where labor mobility costs are high tend to obstruct trade more than countries with more nimble labor markets. Perhaps this is because countries are aware of the short- to medium-term costs to workers of opening industries to competition.

Figure 3.2 Labor Mobility Costs Are Correlated with Country Characteristics

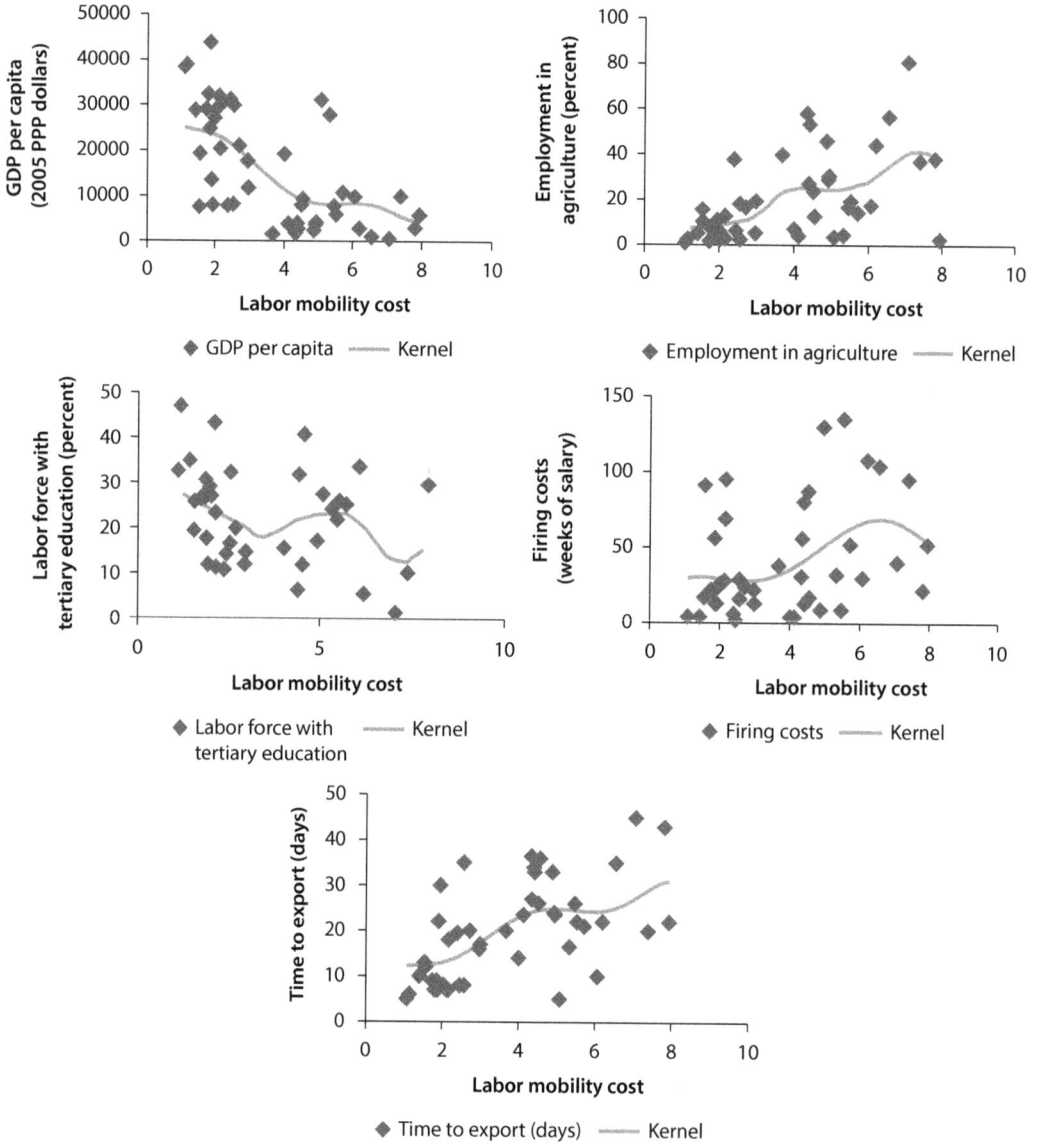

Source: Artuç, Lederman, and Porto 2013.
Note: Figure 3.2 plots bivariate nonparametric regressions between various country characteristics (vertical axis) and the magnitude of the estimated labor mobility costs *C* (horizontal axis) for each country in the sample. Employment in agriculture and the labor force with tertiary education are measured as a percentage of the population. Firing costs are measured as weeks of wages. All variables are from the World Bank's *World Development Indicators*, using averages for 1995–2007. Of the five variables shown, firing costs affecting firms are the least correlated with mobility costs.

Mobility Costs in Action: Simulations of Adjustment Dynamics

Using estimates of labor mobility costs, the analytical framework makes it possible to explore the potential impact of a trade shock on a specific sector, what happens to wages and employment in that sector (i.e., how many workers decide to switch sectors), and how other sectors respond. This analytical approach is reflected in the Trade and Labor Adjustment Costs Toolkit developed by the World Bank International Trade Department. Simulating these adjustment dynamics can help guide policy responses to trade-related shocks by allowing analysts to assess ex ante how labor markets will respond to liberalization that has not yet been implemented, for example, or how labor markets will respond to price changes emanating from international markets.

To simulate the adjustment dynamics of worker transitions between industries over time when labor mobility is costly, the analysis uses an equilibrium model in which the structure of the economy is specified using assumptions about the production function in each sector as well as demand functions and their parameters. Parameters are calculated using data on labor and consumption shares across sectors of the economy (generally available from input-output tables). The production and demand functions are then used to calibrate the initial steady state of the economy. After an economy is hit by the trade shock, the path to the new steady state of wages and employment can be simulated in the affected sector and the other sectors of the economy.[7] As an illustration, the analysis uses an exogenous and unexpected 30 percent decline in the output price of the food and beverage sector due to a tariff reduction.[8]

Separate simulations have been performed for all countries in the database, a subset of which is presented in figure 3.3. Each graph shows the proportional change in average real wages and employment by sector after a 30 percent decline in the price of food and beverages. (The analysis does not allow for movements into or out of unemployment or the labor force, but this assumption is relaxed below.)

This equilibrium analysis illustrates how a trade-related shock affects jobs and wages not only in the liberalized sector but in the rest of the economy as well due to shifts in relative labor demand and supply. Taking Indonesia as an example, the simulation of a 30 percent decline in food and beverage prices causes an immediate real wage cut of 14.8 percent in year 1, followed by full recovery to the initial level by year 5 and ultimately a net wage increase of 17.4 percent in the new steady state 12 years after the shock. At the same time, the initial wage cut leads to significant labor shedding in the sector (12 percent by year 2, 22 percent by year 5) and a reallocation to other sectors. Some of the workers transition to other manufacturing, where employment eventually increases by 6.8 percent; others transition into the nonmanufacturing residual sector, but the net inflow represents a very small fraction of the very large residual sector, which is why figure 3.3 shows no detectable impact.[9] Real wages outside the food and beverage sector both increase significantly post-shock due to increased purchasing power because food and beverages cost less, but the subsequent inflow of labor into other manufacturing pulls the wage down somewhat as the labor market adjusts.

Despite cross-country variations in the estimated magnitudes and speed of adjustment, the following general trends can be seen in response to the shock.

- *Workers in the liberalized sector see real wages decline and workers in all other sectors see real wages rise immediately after the trade reform.* In all countries,

Figure 3.3 Average Real Wages Tend to Recover after Trade Liberalization but Take Time to Return to Steady State

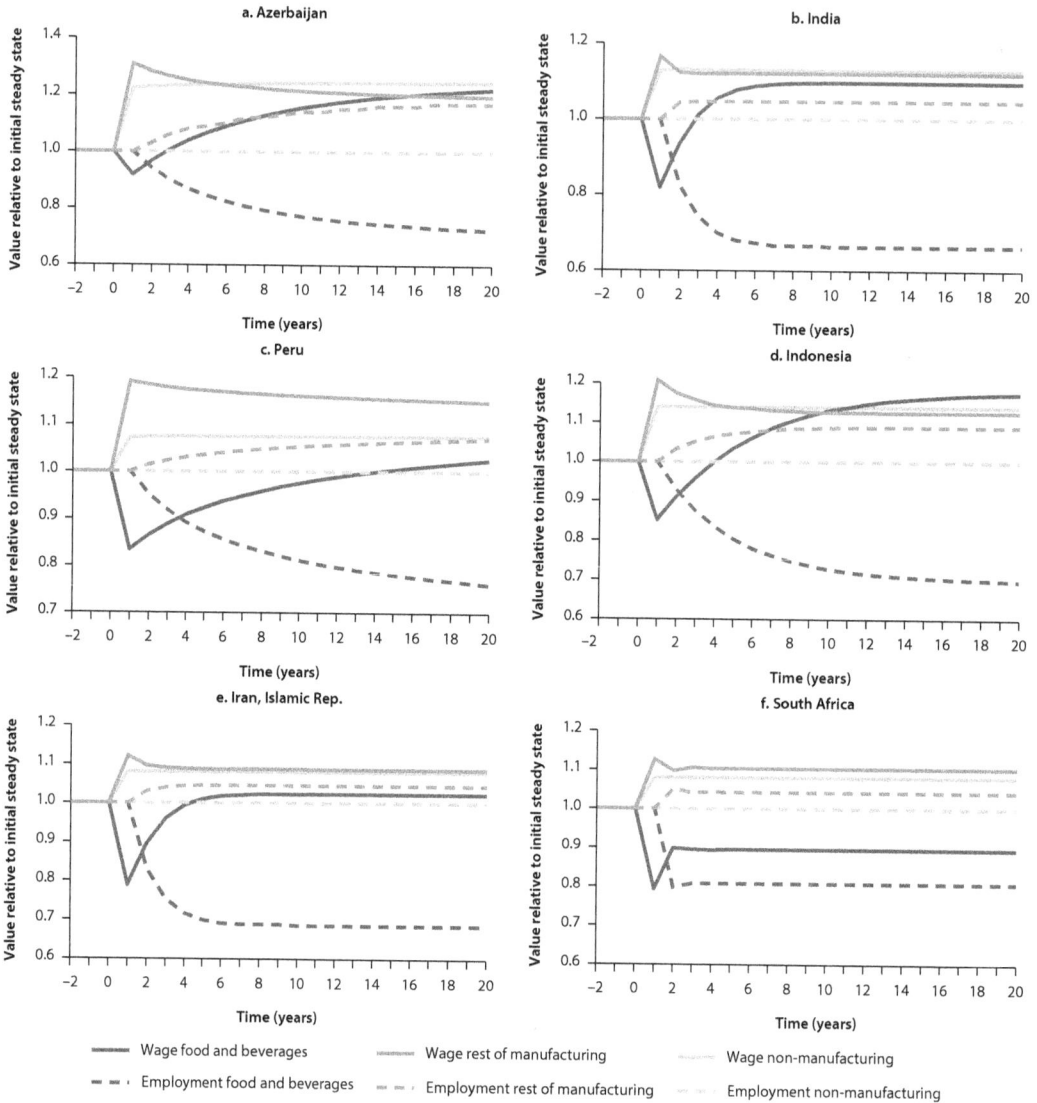

Legend:

——— Wage food and beverages   ········ Wage rest of manufacturing   ········ Wage non-manufacturing

– – – Employment food and beverages   – – – Employment rest of manufacturing   – – – Employment non-manufacturing

Source: Artuç, Lederman, and Porto 2013.
Note: Figure 3.3 shows simulations of labor market responses to a 30 percent price decline in food and beverages. Each graph shows on the vertical axis the proportional change relative to the initial steady state of average real wages (solid lines) and employment (dashed lines) for the food and beverage sector, the remaining manufacturing sectors, and the nonmanufacturing sector. The horizontal axis measures time ($t = 0$ is the date of trade liberalization). Although workers in the liberalized sector experience declines in real wages for all countries immediately after the trade reform, in most cases real wages recover to a new and higher steady state.

the decrease in the price of food and beverages causes a loss of profitability and translates into lower nominal wages in the sector. The decline in the economy's price index (CPI) is proportional to the food and beverages share (less than one). Constant nominal wages elsewhere together with lower prices cause real wages of workers in the rest of the economy to increase because their purchasing power is higher. There are sizable differences in these initial responses (see, e.g., Azerbaijan versus the Islamic Republic of Iran) because the weight of food in the price index varies by country.

- *These wage changes incentivize labor to reallocate between sectors.* The resulting changes in intersectoral wage differentials create incentives for workers to move out of food and beverages and into sectors where real wages have risen.

- *These labor reallocations have implications for wages, which are generally higher for workers in the affected sector in the new steady state.* After the initial increase, over time the real wage in other manufacturing sectors gradually declines as workers move in. However, in the new steady state real wages are always higher than in the initial steady state. Similarly, real wages of workers in the liberalized sector gradually rise as workers move out. It is remarkable that, in most cases, real wages actually recover and are in fact higher in the new steady state than before the shock. There are only four exceptions: Costa Rica, Latvia, Romania, and South Africa. Moreover, the large size of the residual sector means that any labor inflows would have minimal additional effect on the sectoral equilibrium wage.

- *The adjustment period can be very long, particularly for countries with high labor mobility costs.* It can take more than 10 years to reach the new steady state in many countries, although wages in the affected sector tend to recover in less than 5 years. In Azerbaijan and India, for example, the recovery occurs within 2 years of the initial wage decline, but in Peru it takes 12 years. This supports the assertion that lost earnings are a main preoccupation of workers affected by trade-related shocks, since they may recover their relative earnings only after a long period of time.[10] Worldwide, the average speed of convergence to the new steady state is 5.44 years in developing countries, 2.5 years in developed countries. The convergence period lengthens as mobility costs rise.[11]

In summary, an average worker who faces an exogenous negative wage shock and who is stuck for a given period in the liberalized sector bears the brunt of the adjustment costs, but these short-term costs are ultimately offset by gains from future higher wages. However, there are several important caveats to keep in mind: Not all affected sectors recover, as illustrated by South Africa, where wages in the food and beverage sector remain depressed by 11 percent in the new equilibrium. The specification assumes no labor reallocation to unemployment or out of the labor force (this assumption is relaxed below). By focusing on manufacturing, the impact on the residual nonmanufacturing sector may be understated in developing countries with large informal sectors. Because the price shock illustrated is in the food and beverages sector, the positive impact on real wages in other sectors due to higher purchasing power is significant because of the disproportionate weight of food and beverages in a worker's consumption basket. Repeating the analysis for a trade shock in the textile sector,

Artuç, Lederman, and Porto (2013) found significant wage and employment losses for the average worker in developing countries with large textile industries, which suggests that the overall impact of trade liberalization in the textile sector would be different.

Labor Adjustment Costs: How Much Are Workers Losing Out?

Labor mobility costs reduce both the speed of transition to the new steady state and the gains from trade. Their magnitude determines the response to a shock: the higher the mobility cost, the longer the time it takes to transition to the new steady state. In general, labor market responses are sluggish because mobility costs create frictions, especially in the sector affected.

How can the welfare losses resulting from labor mobility costs be quantified? These losses—the labor adjustment costs—are calculated as the difference in aggregate worker welfare between *optimal* labor allocations after a trade shock (i.e., with instantaneous adjustment when mobility costs are zero) and *actual* labor allocations (when mobility costs are positive). The magnitude of adjustment costs depends not only on the magnitude of the mobility costs but also on the specific country context. Adjustment costs are estimated using the simulated labor adjustment dynamics after a trade-related shock that were previously described. The adjustment dynamics of the transition from the pre-shock steady state to the post-shock steady state produce estimates of worker welfare associated with predicted labor market outcomes. Labor adjustment costs are calculated by solving for this welfare when there are mobility costs and comparing it to welfare when the costs are zero.

The concepts of adjustment costs and gains from trade after liberalization of a sector are defined more formally as follows (see appendix A for more detail):

- The initial welfare of a worker in the affected sector is denoted by V_{pre}. If there are no mobility costs, the welfare of the worker will increase instantaneously from the pre-shock steady-state level, V_{pre}, to the post-shock steady-state level, V_{max}. The increase captures the *potential* gains from trade.
- However, if there are mobility costs, the adjustment is sluggish and the worker will incur an immediate change in welfare due to changes in the option value and the real wage and a subsequent increase in welfare during the transition to the new steady state. The actual welfare value achieved in the post-shock steady state by a worker who starts off in the affected sector is denoted V. The *actual* gains are the difference between V and V_{pre}.
- The difference between the potential and the actual gains is the *labor adjustment cost* (or forgone gains to trade).

Given the magnitude and cross-country variation of labor mobility costs, labor adjustment costs could be expected to be large and to vary across countries; this is borne out by the estimates based on a 30 percent decline in the output price of food and beverages. The welfare gains (see appendix C, columns 2–4) represent a lower bound of economy-wide welfare gains because they refer to workers in the negatively affected sector. Moreover, the analysis does not allow for dynamic gains through, for example, productivity enhancement as firms learn from exporting or adoption of technology as they learn from importing.

For workers in the liberalized food and beverage sector, actual gains from trade liberalization tend to be positive and large. For developing countries, the *gains from trade even for workers in the negatively affected sector are equivalent to at least 5.2 percent of workers' initial welfare.*[12] Although real wages in the food and beverage sector decline initially, the decline is usually temporary. In addition, the higher option value of future labor choices of a worker stuck in the sector also raises the worker's overall welfare due to increases in real wages in the rest of the economy. Among developing countries, only in Peru would workers in the sector lose out from lower prices (because of high mobility costs and a long recovery period). Overall, the net welfare effect is positive, which suggests that trade liberalization is welfare-improving in the new equilibrium even in the sector hit by the negative price shock.

Countries would gain even more from a decline in food and beverage prices if there were no labor mobility costs. The simulations confirm that potential gains from trade (i.e., the welfare gains in the absence of labor mobility costs) for workers in the affected sector are always positive, although magnitudes vary from a very low 0.55 percent of initial welfare in the United States to almost 20 percent in Azerbaijan. For developing countries, the potential gains to trade average 7.5 percent of initial welfare (see appendix C).

As mobility costs increase, so do adjustment costs, but the increase is not linear. Because developing countries have higher mobility costs, they also suffer higher adjustment costs. Singapore, for example, has mobility costs of only 1.09 times the annual average wage, and the labor adjustment cost is 0.07 percent of the initial welfare. But for Peru, which has the highest estimated mobility cost, the adjustment cost is equivalent to 7.25 percent of initial welfare. The average adjustment cost for food and beverage workers in developing countries is 2.3 percent of initial welfare.

When adjustment costs are expressed as a share of total gains from trade (consistent with the literature),[13] the forgone gains to trade due to frictions in labor mobility can be substantial. Average forgone gains for developing countries are equivalent to about one-third of the potential gains. But the forgone gains can be extremely high in countries like Turkey (92 percent of potential gains to trade) and Chile (84 percent) (see appendix C, last two columns). Even in countries where labor mobility costs are modest, the forgone gains imply significant opportunity costs. In the United States, for example, the forgone gains are estimated at 11 percent of potential and 12 percent of actual gains. Figure 3.4 illustrates the range of forgone gains from trade (labor adjustment costs as a share of potential gains) and their correlation with mobility costs for the entire sample.[14]

Figure 3.4 Forgone Gains from Trade Rise with Mobility Costs

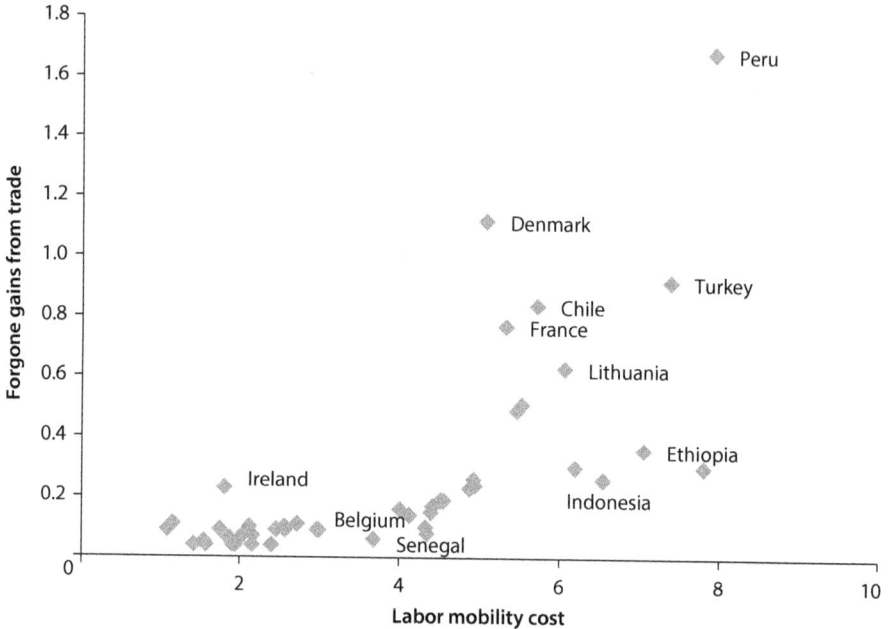

Source: Artuç, Lederman, and Porto 2013.
Note: Figure 3.4 plots on the vertical axis estimated forgone gains from trade for each country measured as the ratio of
the labor adjustment cost to potential gains from trade. The horizontal axis measures labor mobility costs as a ratio of the
annual average wage.

Notes

1. Based on Artuç, Chaudhuri, and McLaren (2010).

2. A worker deciding between more than two sectors would compare the expected
   welfare of staying in the current sector with that of the sector that provides the
   maximum discounted welfare net of moving costs.

3. The C curves represent the cumulative distribution of workers that move for a
   given cost, including the idiosyncratic shocks faced by the worker, $C + \varepsilon^{i,j}$. The shape
   of curves C_1 and C_2 is determined by the assumed distribution of the worker-specific
   costs ε.

4. Chapter 3 presents the *average* mobility cost estimated for each country, whereas
   chapter 4 presents the estimated mobility costs disaggregated by sector and by formality status and firm size within each sector. That is, for each worker the costs of moving
   depend on the worker's potential future sector of work, type of firm, informality
   status, etc. The analytical framework remains the same, however.

5. Net flows of workers refer to the number of workers in each sector of the economy
   at each point in time. Gross flows refer to the number of workers *transitioning* from
   each sector of the economy to all other sectors.

6. There is no evidence of a correlation between mobility costs and primary or secondary education, possibly because there is less variance across countries in the
   sample in terms of the percentage of the population with primary or secondary
   education.

7. See appendix A and Artuç, Chaudhuri, and McLaren (2008, 2010) for details on the structure of the simulations and algorithms used to solve the model. This involves computing the perfect-foresight path of the adjustment from the liberalization announcement until the economy has effectively reached the new steady state. This requires—taking the time path of wages in all sectors as given—that each worker optimally decides at each date whether or not to switch sectors, taking into account personal idiosyncratic shocks. Because this induces a time path for the allocation of workers, it also generates the time path of wages, since the wage in each sector at each date is determined by the market-clearing conditions given the number of workers currently in the sector.

8. The following are assumed in order to simulate the effects of a trade-related shock: (1) without loss of generality, units are chosen so that the domestic price of each good at date $t = -1$ is unity; (2) there are no tariffs at any date on any sector other than the food and beverage sector; (3) the world price of food and beverages is 0.7 at each date and the price of all other tradable goods is unity; (4) there is initially a tariff on food and beverages of 0.3 per unit, so that the domestic price of food and beverages is equal to unity; (5) initially the tariff is expected to be permanent and the economy reaches steady state with that expectation; (6) at date $t = -1$, however, after the period's decisions about moving have been made, the government announces that the tariff will be removed beginning at date $t = 0$ (so the domestic price of food and beverages will fall from unity to 0.7 at that date), and this liberalization is permanent. For simplicity, 100 percent price pass-through of the tariff change is assumed, but this assumption can be relaxed.

9. The employment share of the food and beverage sector falls from 0.74 percent in the pre-shock steady state to 0.52 percent in the new steady state. The share of other manufacturing sectors rises from 2.9 to 3.1 percent, but the employment share of nonmanufacturing activities increases only very marginally, from 96.38 percent pre-shock to 96.41 percent in the new steady state.

10. This result is consistent with Krebs, Krishna, and Maloney (2010), who identify large short-run reductions in the welfare of workers in the affected sector after a trade shock.

11. For estimated labor mobility costs of up to about four times the annual wage, the convergence speed is constant at two years. This includes most developed countries. For mobility costs greater than four times the annual wage, the length of convergence time increases steeply with the costs.

12. This estimate refers to a random food and beverage worker who experienced the negative shock. Workers in the rest of the economy always gain from lower prices for food and beverages. This estimate therefore reflects a lower bound.

13. Davidson and Matusz (2010).

14. The ratio of forgone to potential gains from a negative shock in food and beverages is greater than one in countries where the actual gains to trade are negative, namely in Peru and Denmark.

References

Artuç, E., S. Chaudhuri, and J. McLaren. 2008. "Delay and Dynamics in Labor Market Adjustment: Simulation Results." *Journal of International Economics* 75 (1): 1–13.

———. 2010. "Trade Shocks and Labor Adjustment: A Structural Empirical Approach." *American Economic Review* 100: 1008–45.

Artuç, E., D. Lederman, and G. Porto. 2013. "A Mapping of Labor Mobility Costs in the Developing World." Policy Research Working Paper 6556, World Bank, Washington, DC.

Davidson, C., and S. J. Matusz. 2010. *International Trade with Equilibrium Unemployment.* Princeton, NJ: Princeton University Press.

Krebs, T., P. Krishna, and W. Maloney. 2010. "Trade Policy, Income Risk, and Welfare." *Review of Economics and Statistics* 92 (3): 467–81.

CHAPTER 4

Mobility Costs, Adjustment Costs, and Employment Structure in Developing Economies: Four Case Studies

Abstract

The Argentine case study examines how firms adjust their capital and labor after a negative price shock when capital adjustment costs are high, and finds that costly capital adjustment only mildly affects firm decisions about hiring and firing and that larger shocks tend to benefit profits proportionately more than workers' wages.

When labor mobility costs are disaggregated by sector to compare developed and developing country labor market responses to trade shocks, although formal workers in Mexico and the United States exhibit similar degrees of mobility, the costs are much higher in Mexico, where workers are more likely to move for nonwage reasons.

For developing countries, informal employment acts as a stepping stone to obtaining a formal job. It is relatively less costly to move to a formal job from an informal job in the same industry, and workers face the highest moving costs when transitioning from informal work in one industry to formal work in another. Given the lower entry costs to informality, tariff liberalization that pushes down domestic prices can lead to increased informal employment drawn primarily from previously inactive or unemployed workers.

Firm size appears to affect labor mobility costs. Evidence from Morocco shows that finding employment in large firms is easier than in small firms, which suggests that workers affected by a negative trade shock are more likely to transition into jobs in large rather than small firms.

Developing economies and their labor markets are very different from those of developed economies; so labor mobility and adjustment costs may be expected to differ as well. For example, institutional and regulatory settings in developed economies translate into easier access to finance, insurance, and other mechanisms that support private sector growth, as well as increased regulatory oversight and worker protections. In contrast, weaker institutions in developing economies translate into much more informality and greater disparity in the operational and incentive structures of firms.

This chapter uses country case studies as a basis for disaggregated approaches to estimating labor mobility and adjustment costs for post-shock worker transitions. Mobility costs are estimated for different types of workers transitioning within and between sectors and are then further disaggregated by formality status and firm size. Country mobility cost estimates averaged over all sectors in chapter 3 are useful for cross-country comparisons and exploit readily available data on net job flows between sectors, but they cannot capture variations in worker behavior determined by sectoral, firm, or worker characteristics. The analytical framework underlying the Trade and Labor Adjustment Costs Toolkit presented in chapter 3 is extended here to panel data on workers in which gross—rather than net—job flows across industries can be observed. The analysis below illustrates applications of the toolkit to developing countries using data from, for example, social security records and household and labor force surveys to generate disaggregated sector-specific mobility costs, which are used to simulate labor market responses to a trade-related shock and the resulting adjustment costs. The case studies highlight not only the broad scope of the methodology—making it possible to address a range of policy questions—but also the importance of accounting for heterogeneity.

Firm Costs versus Worker Costs: The Case of Argentina

Faced with a negative demand shock, how do firms balance the costs of capital adjustment and labor adjustment, and what are the costs to workers in terms of employment and wages? The case study of Argentina by Artuç et al. (2013) considers adjustments firms might make after a shock in terms of reallocating labor or capital. On the one hand, if capital adjustment is costly, a firm may respond by adjusting its labor force. The evidence presented in chapter 2 showed that labor is the more viable factor of adjustment for firms facing trade-related price shocks. On the other hand, the firm may choose not to make a capital adjustment if the costs outweigh the benefits, in which case workers may be less affected. Argentina is used as a case study to answer this question by modeling both costly capital adjustment and costly labor mobility for workers.

The case study assesses the implications for workers of costly and lumpy capital adjustment as translated through labor demand. This first attempt at combining the two adjustment cost literature streams discussed in chapter 2 combines the labor supply model characterized by workers' sectoral employment choices developed by Artuç, Chaudhuri, and McLaren (2010) with the labor demand model characterized by capital adjustment costs presented by Cooper and Haltiwanger (2006). On the supply side, workers face costly labor mobility. On the demand side, firms face costs to adjusting their capital stock, both convex and fixed investment costs and investment irreversibility costs. Convex costs induce firms to smooth investment over time; non-convex fixed costs create occasional investment bursts—lumpy adjustment. Investment irreversibility costs arise when installed capital can only be sold at a fraction of the purchase price. Faced with an exogenous price shock, firms make intertemporal profit-maximizing decisions and workers make welfare-maximizing sectoral employment choices. The model is estimated using firm- and household-level survey panel data from Argentina to recover the structural parameters characterizing the frictions that firms and workers must both deal with, namely, capital adjustment costs and labor mobility costs.[1]

For Argentina, the results show large costs of capital adjustment, supporting the evidence in previous studies that firms are inflexible when adjusting capital. The fixed cost of adjustment is significant, estimated to be equivalent to 14.5 percent of average plant-level capital value. Convex adjustment costs are 0.056 percent of average plant-level capital, and resale of capital goods would incur a loss of about 8.6 percent of the original purchase price. These estimates are all larger than those found for the United States by Cooper and Haltiwanger (2006), which suggests that capital is less flexible in Argentina. On the supply side, a worker in Argentina wishing to switch sectors within manufacturing would pay an average mobility cost equivalent to 2.07 times annual wage earnings—a relatively high cost for workers compared to firms.

Because these capital adjustment costs cause the economy to react partially and gradually to a trade-related shock, they have implications for labor demand, employment, and wages. The magnitude of capital adjustment costs affects firm investment behavior: depending on the cost, firms may enter periods of investment, disinvestment, or inaction (maintaining the status quo). When a trade shock is positive, some firms will be moved out of inaction and into investment. The economy thus adjusts. But many other firms will remain inactive, especially if the costs of capital adjustment are high. To explore the impact of an exogenous trade-related shock when both capital adjustment and labor mobility are costly, a 10 percent increase in the price of food and beverages output is assumed. This type of price increase could result from, for example, a tariff increase in the sector or increases in global food prices due to external supply shocks. Figure 4.1 illustrates simulations of the adjustment dynamics of wages, employment, capital, and output in the food and beverage sector. The immediate implication of higher prices is an increase in profitability for producers, so firms will want to expand and invest. However, since capital adjustment is costly, their stock of capital goes up only gradually. Three fourths of the capital adjustment to the new steady state takes place within five years after the trade shock, and 95 percent of the transition occurs within nine years. Thus output also increases gradually.

The labor market also responds sluggishly. Real wages increase at first in the food and beverage sector but decline elsewhere due to the higher prices. As wages change, workers gradually transition toward the food and beverage sector, but the influx of labor drives wages down again, although they stay above

Figure 4.1 Argentina's Sluggish Economic Responses under Costly Capital and Labor Adjustment

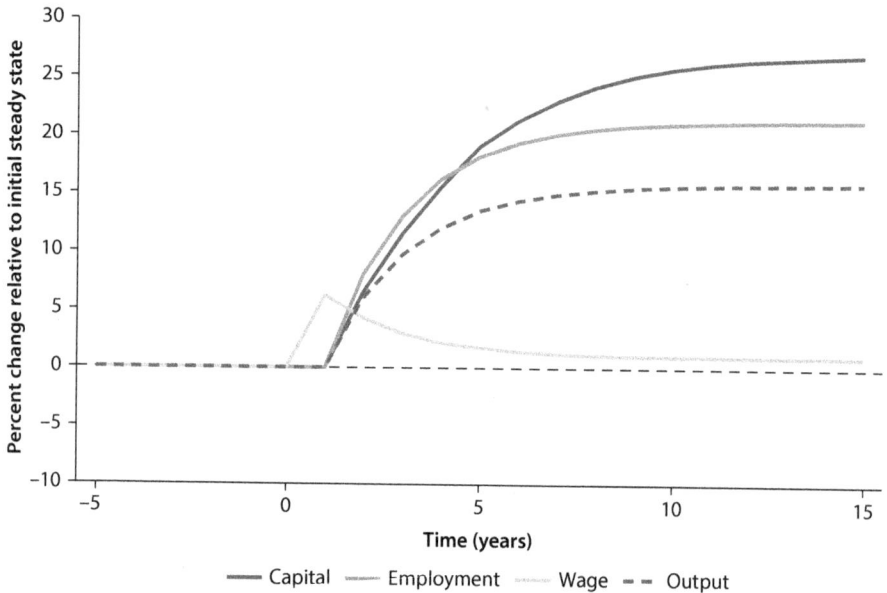

Source: Artuç et al. 2013.

Note: Figure 4.1 shows the simulated adjustment paths of wages, employment, capital, and output in the food and beverage sector after a 10 percent increase in output price when there are capital adjustment and labor mobility costs. The vertical axis plots the percent change relative to the initial steady state for each variable, and the horizontal axis measures time where time $t = 0$ represents the year of the price change.

the pre-shock steady-state level. Meanwhile, real wages in all other sectors recover slightly.[2]

Costly and lumpy capital adjustment only mildly affects firm decisions about hiring and firing. The response of employment is only slightly higher and wages slightly lower when there are no firm-level adjustment costs of capital. The dynamic paths of wages, employment, and capital depend on the degree of capital adjustment costs and the possibility of inaction.

To explore this dependence, counterfactual simulations are performed where there is a 10 percent positive shock to the price of food and beverages but with no fixed costs of investment or irreversibility costs. Table 4.1 shows the levels of capital, wages, and employment for the food and beverage sector without such costs as ratios to their levels when there are costs. The ratios are shown for various years throughout the adjustment period and the post-shock steady state. The capital stock adjusts much more sharply and quickly if there are no adjustment costs; the presence of adjustment costs generates investment inaction by firms for four to five years after a trade shock.[3] But in the long run, total adjustment is similar; the absence of capital adjustment costs results in only marginally higher capital investment in the steady state. For example, the response of capital in the second year after the shock is 55 percent larger if there are no adjustment costs,

Table 4.1 Firm Behavior with and without Capital Adjustment Costs:
Firms Adjust Capital by More, and More Quickly without Adjustment Costs,
but Not Labor

	Capital	Wages	Employment
Year 1	1.000	1.001	1.000
Year 2	1.554	−1.031	1.031
Year 3	1.459	−1.023	1.028
Year 4	1.337	−1.009	1.028
Year 5	1.240	−1.004	1.029
Year 10	1.066	−1.008	1.029
Steady state	1.032	−1.013	1.026

Source: Artuç et al. 2013.

Note: Table 4.1 shows the levels of capital, wages, and employment for the food and beverage sector in the absence of both fixed costs of investment and irreversibility costs as a ratio of the levels when such costs are present. The levels are shown for the years after a 10 percent increase in food and beverage prices, and for the post-shock steady state. The results indicate more rapid and larger capital adjustment without adjustment costs, but little effect on employment and wages.

but only 3 percent larger in the steady state. Although for capital there are large differences in the short-run responses, that is not the case for wages or employment. The short-run responses of employment are slightly stronger if there are no capital adjustment costs (3 percent in the second year after the shock) but never as pronounced as the response of the capital stock. Real wages therefore react less in the short run, meaning that wages always increase but proportionally less when there are no fixed costs to investment or irreversibility costs.

Larger shocks tend to benefit firm profits proportionally more than worker wages; this has implications for the distributional gains from trade. The dynamic paths of wages, employment, capital, and output depend also on the size of the shock. As expected, the economy adjusts more when the trade shock is larger. As the positive price shock becomes larger, the aggregate capital stock of the economy becomes proportionally more responsive, as does output. This happens because higher price changes make factor adjustment profitable even if it is costly, so that a larger proportion of firms move from inaction to investment. However, this enhanced responsiveness of capital to larger shocks is not reflected in the responsiveness of employment or real wages. The proportional adjustment of real wages is instead independent of the size of the shock. The implication is that *firms gain relatively more than workers from positive trade-related shocks.*

Labor Mobility Costs across Industries: The Case of Mexico

What factors cause labor mobility and adjustment costs to vary in different industries? Access to Mexican social security data, which spans all economic activity in the formal economy, makes it possible to expand the analysis to explore how mobility costs vary across broad sectors of the economy (an approach developed by Kaplan, Lederman, and Robertson 2013 in a study commissioned for this report). These findings could help inform policymakers about which industries are more difficult for workers to access and help to identify possible underlying factors. In addition, by following the same methodology used by Artuç, Chaudhuri, and McLaren (2010), the analysis can compare costs for Mexico and the United States.[4]

There is significant heterogeneity in mobility costs for workers entering different industries, and the costs may be positively related to the amount of specific versus general skills necessary for employment in the new industry. The findings also support the chapter 3 conclusion that worker mobility costs can be quite significant in developing countries, especially compared to those in developed countries; that highlights the importance of accounting for mobility costs when estimating the impact of trade-related shocks on labor market outcomes.

Although the rates of formal worker transitions between sectors in Mexico are comparable to those in the United States, Mexican workers seem less responsive to wage differentials, which suggests that mobility costs are high. The transition statistics reported in table 4.2 indicate that formal labor market flows in Mexico and the United States are similar in magnitude. Whereas exclusion of informal workers in the Mexico data is likely to understate the actual number of within- and between-sector worker transitions, the shares of workers transitioning between sectors may be only marginally affected.[5] Net inflows to manufacturing can be seen from agriculture, construction, transport and trade, and net outflows from manufacturing to the service industries.

Despite similar estimates of labor flows, however, mobility costs in Mexico are 6–10 times larger than in the United States. Although Mexican firm adjustment costs are an order of magnitude smaller than those estimated in the United States (Robertson and Dutkowsky 2002), estimates of both the labor mobility costs (C) and the variance (v) of the idiosyncratic mobility costs (ε) are substantially higher in Mexico (illustrated in table 4.3 for different values of the worker's discount factor, β).[6] Whereas it is assumed that human capital in developing countries is less specific, and thus more adaptable, than in the United States, U.S. workers on average have more general skills even if they are also on average hyper-specialized (general skills are a prerequisite for obtaining specialized skills). While U.S. workers would also expect a decline in their wages if changing industries, their wider skill set in general, such as computer skills or greater reading and writing comprehension, makes it easier for them to move between jobs than for workers in developing countries like Mexico. Thus it would be expected that mobility costs would be lower in the United States.

Mobility costs are also higher in Mexico because Mexican workers are more likely to move for nonwage reasons. For example, according to recent household survey data 86 percent of the workers who voluntarily separated from their last job left for marriage or family care reasons (Kaplan, Lederman, and Robertson 2013). The higher values of v in Mexico imply that nonpecuniary factors are much more important. In fact, wages in Mexico are generally about 10 percent of wages in the United States. Interestingly, the ratio C/v is roughly the same

Table 4.2 Gross Flows of Formal Sector Workers across Industries Are Similar in the United States and Mexico

	United States						Mexico					
	Agriculture/ mining	Construction	Manufacturing	Transport/ utilities	Trade	Services	Agriculture/ mining	Construction	Manufacturing	Transport/ utilities	Trade	Services
Agriculture/mining	0.9292	0.0126	0.0142	0.0075	0.0160	0.0206	0.9209	0.0154	0.0284	0.0053	0.0142	0.0158
Construction	0.0056	0.9432	0.0139	0.0063	0.0119	0.0191	0.0075	0.8626	0.0500	0.0095	0.0273	0.0431
Manufacturing	0.0020	0.0041	0.9708	0.0031	0.0080	0.0120	0.0020	0.0086	0.9400	0.0044	0.0232	0.0218
Transport/utilities	0.0025	0.0044	0.0068	0.9643	0.0081	0.0138	0.0019	0.0070	0.0187	0.9263	0.0189	0.0272
Trade	0.0030	0.0061	0.0135	0.0055	0.9469	0.0250	0.0018	0.0081	0.0394	0.0075	0.8995	0.0437
Services	0.0018	0.0043	0.0079	0.0037	0.0103	0.9720	0.0014	0.0078	0.0258	0.0065	0.0270	0.9316

Sources: Artuç, Chaudhuri, and McLaren 2010; Kaplan, Lederman, and Robertson 2013.

Note: Using social security data on formal sector workers in Mexico, table 4.2 reports the average share of workers transitioning from each origin sector (rows) to all other destination sectors (columns). The stayers, which appear on the diagonal, are the largest group. U.S. data are from the Census Bureau's annual March Current Population Surveys. The country datasets are broadly comparable because the share of informal workers in the United States is very small.

(between 4 and 5) for Mexico and the United States, which is consistent with the fact that their gross flows of workers are not very different. What is different, however, is that formal Mexican workers seem much less responsive to wage differentials across industries, which could reflect strong preferences for formal employment and the less dynamic job creation observed in the formal sector (Bosch and Maloney 2007). These mobility cost estimates are substantially higher than the average mobility costs reported in chapter 3 (for the United States, C is only 1.16 times the average annual wage [see appendix C] compared to 8–13 times the average annual wage in table 4.3); this discrepancy is explained by differences in the level of sectoral disaggregation.

Other factors that raise mobility costs in less developed countries are not explicitly captured in these measures. These include barriers to entry into self-employment due to difficulty accessing capital. Because the market for formal wage jobs is thinner in developing countries, the relatively privileged set of wage workers may perceive a higher risk in moving to a new sector or job, particularly in single-earner households.[7] Wages also tend to be more volatile in developing countries; if workers are risk averse and anticipate this volatility, they may be less likely to change jobs in response to wage shocks. If foreign-owned firms pay above-market average wages, mobility costs may be larger in countries with high levels of foreign direct investment. Finally, if industries are more regionally concentrated in developing countries, for example, with large agriculture sectors located in remote rural areas and manufacturing in the cities, the mobility cost of physically relocating would be higher.

While the estimates suggest that on average workers in Mexico perceive the costs of moving between sectors to be high, there is heterogeneity across industries. This means that for a given wage gap between industries, some industries receive more worker flows than others. From a policy perspective, this highlights the importance of considering labor mobility costs at the industry rather than the aggregate level. Table 4.4 presents estimated labor mobility costs for entering different industries in Mexico expressed as a ratio of average annual wage earnings. Given the nature of Mexican social security data, if an employee leaves the formal (tax-registered) sector, it is not possible to know whether the employee becomes unemployed, leaves the labor force, or finds a job in the informal sector. To address this, the methodology assumes that individuals who leave the formal

Table 4.3 Labor Mobility Costs Are Higher in Mexico than the United States

	$\beta = 0.97$		$\beta = 0.90$	
	United States	*Mexico*	*United States*	*Mexico*
v	2.897	22.862	1.600	46.211
C	13.210	81.988	7.699	180.112

Sources: Artuç, Chaudhuri, and McLaren 2010; Kaplan, Lederman, and Robertson 2013.
Note: Table 4.3 shows estimates of both labor mobility costs (*C*), expressed as a ratio of average annual wage earnings, and the variance of the idiosyncratic mobility costs (*v*) for Mexico (from Kaplan, Lederman, and Robertson 2013) and comparable estimates for the United States (from Artuç, Chaudhuri, and McLaren 2010) for different values of the worker's discount factor, *β*.

Table 4.4 Labor Mobility Costs in Mexico: Do Skills Play a Role?

v	2.585
C—Agriculture/mining	15.306
C—Construction	8.197
C—Manufacturing	9.205
C—Transportation/communications/utilities	14.490
C—Trade (wholesale and retail)	9.700
C—Services	9.455

Source: Kaplan, Lederman, and Robertson 2013.
Note: Table 4.4 reports Mexican labor mobility costs of entering different industries (the average for workers from all other industries in the economy), expressed as a ratio of average annual wage earnings, estimated for each year between 1997 and 2004, and averaged across all years. The estimation strategy follows Artuç 2013.

sector enter the residual sector, and their wages are approximated using wages of informal workers from household surveys.[8] While the estimated labor mobility costs of entering an industry (the average for workers from all other industries in the economy) are lower in table 4.4 than in table 4.3, they are still much higher than estimates for the United States.[9]

The mobility costs of entering an industry may rise with respect to the amount of "specific" skills necessary for employment in that industry. Industries with the lowest entry costs for formal workers seem to be consistent with those requiring general rather than specific skills (e.g., construction, services, and retail and wholesale trade) and thus are more accessible. Industries with the highest entry costs, by contrast, namely formal-sector agriculture, transportation/communications, and utilities, may require more specialized skills. (While informal agricultural employment is not likely to require specific skills, to be employed as a formal agricultural worker in Mexico is likely to be skill-intensive, because these workers include, for example, engineers and managers. The costs to entering informal agricultural employment are in fact low, as illustrated below.) The data needed to test the correlation with skill level are lacking.

Note that the level of industry classification affects the magnitude of the estimates. This is a crucial methodological issue that needs to be taken into account in this type of research. Excessive disaggregation of industry levels can produce counter-intuitive results: the magnitude of labor mobility costs rises when industries are more disaggregated, even though it should be easier to move between two subsectors of manufacturing that use similar skills than to move, for example, between manufacturing and nonmanufacturing sectors.[10] But this result is a mechanical byproduct of this measurement approach. The analysis estimates adjustment costs using data on observed worker transitions between industries, so that the magnitude of these flows depends on the degree of industry disaggregation—the greater the disaggregation, the fewer the transitions, the higher the mobility costs.

Before Kaplan, Lederman, and Robertson (2013), there were no careful studies of the robustness of mobility costs across different aggregation levels. For policymakers interested in testing the impact of certain trade shocks, the sector aggregation level selected should correspond to the central issues, namely, whether the costs of moving between different types of manufacturing sectors are more relevant than the costs of moving between agriculture and manufacturing. Wage data in developing countries are also relatively less reliable than data for developed countries. These measurement issues suggest the need for caution in interpreting the precise values of the mobility cost estimates for policy applications.

Role of Informal Employment: The Cases of Brazil, Mexico, and Morocco

Do trade-related shocks affect informal workers differently than formal workers? If the costs of entering informal rather than formal employment are lower, it might be expected that workers displaced by a trade shock would drop into the informal sector, especially in developing countries where informal employment is widespread. Since the term was coined in the early 1970s, the literature has proposed various definitions of "informal employment." From the viewpoint of workers rather than firms, a consensus definition comprises workers who are not covered by social protection, such as social security, or who work without a wage contract (World Bank 2012). Applying this definition to data from labor force surveys, workers who are self-employed or salaried without social security benefits are considered informal.

According to the recent *World Development Report on Jobs* (World Bank 2012), global studies of the incidence of informal employment in the developing world suggest that informality accounts for between 40 and 80 percent of those employed. This estimate is borne out by data from labor force surveys in Brazil, Mexico, and Morocco: informal employment exceeds 40 percent of the labor force in Brazil, is almost 60 percent in Mexico, and is over 80 percent in Morocco (see appendix B for details). This section explores how mobility costs vary between informal and formal workers in different industries in Brazil, Mexico, and Morocco, and generates policy simulations to assess how trade-related shocks will impact labor reallocation and wages across industries and formality status. The results can inform policy in countries where informality is significant.

Trade liberalization that increases real wages can indeed be associated with increases in the share of informal employment, but not because displaced formal workers become informal workers. Rather, as economy-wide employment increases, the observed expansion of informal employment largely comes from workers moving out of the residual sector (unemployed or outside the labor force) into informal employment. Trade-related shocks that permanently reduce domestic prices in developing countries lead to higher real wages, providing incentives for workers to enter the labor force as the opportunity costs of remaining inactive rise. Alternatively, the increase in informal employment could be due to the "added worker" effect in which a second earner may enter the workforce from households hit by income losses. In both cases, workers choose to enter the labor force but mainly informally because entry costs are lower. This result is clear in simulations for Morocco, Mexico, and Brazil elaborated below based on the study by Arias-Vázquez et al. (2013). Whereas informal employment increased after a simulated tariff reduction in those countries, formal employment stayed fairly constant.

The entry point to employment is through the informal sector, which can function as a stepping stone to formality. It is more likely that workers will move in and out of the residual sector of unemployed or outside the labor force than between sectors, highlighting the importance of case studies that can account separately for informality, formality, and unemployment. Gross flows of workers by formality status are shown in table 4.5. Morocco and Mexico show similar patterns for the transition into and out of informality; in both, informal workers are more likely to exit to the residual sector than enter formal employment. In contrast, informality and formality are equally likely entry points for employment in Brazil, and workers in the informal sector are more likely to move to the formal than to the residual sector.

These results are consistent with findings from previous studies that young workers enter employment through the informal salaried sector. In Mexico, Fajnzylber, Maloney, and Montes Rojas (2006) found that informal salaried workers are generally younger and less educated and spend little time in informal employment. Mexican informality is concentrated mainly in services, which tend to have higher turnover (Bosch and Maloney 2007). By contrast, self-employed workers tend to be older, with long tenures of self-employment.

The definition of informal workers in this analysis covers both salaried workers without social protections and self-employed workers, combining two distinct

Table 4.5 Informality as an Entry Point into Employment: Worker Transitions in Morocco, Mexico, and Brazil

Origin/destination	Formal	Informal	Residual	Total
Morocco				
Formal	79.03	13.78	7.19	100.00
Informal	3.42	82.85	13.73	100.00
Residual	0.92	12.03	87.04	100.00
Mexico				
Formal	77.89	14.08	8.03	100.00
Informal	10.46	71.00	18.54	100.00
Residual	5.04	17.95	77.00	100.00
Brazil				
Formal	86.53	4.86	8.61	100.00
Informal	24.63	57.17	18.20	100.00
Residual	8.63	7.15	84.22	100.00

Source: Arias-Vázquez et al. 2013.
Note: Table 4.5 shows gross flows of workers across formality status. It shows the average share of workers transitioning from each origin status (rows) to all other destination statuses (columns). The stayers (on the diagonal) account for the largest share. The residual sector covers both the unemployed and the inactive working-age population.

groups that may behave differently because their mobility costs differ. Indeed, the gross employment flows of the two subgroups do tend to differ. For example, in the United States, being self-employed requires significant financing, human capital, or both (Evans and Jovanovic 1989), implying high entry costs and entry into self-employment later in life compared to entry into informal salaried work (consistent with the evidence for Mexico from Fajnzylber, Maloney, and Montes Rojas 2006). Re-estimating the mobility costs and sectoral adjustment paths for salaried informal workers only (omitting the self-employed) in Mexico and Brazil, in fact, generates very similar results to those presented below; this suggests that the relatively small number of self-employed workers in the sample did not have much impact on labor adjustment patterns. But this caveat should nevertheless be kept in mind when interpreting the results for informal workers.

Certain sectors seem to provide an easier path to informal employment due to lower mobility costs, but those sectors differ by country. It is possible to examine the extent to which differences in mobility costs for informal and formal workers can explain these observed differences in flows between the countries by making a slight adjustment to the framework of the toolkit. The structural model of workers' sectoral employment choices is expanded to incorporate an additional decision about formality status. That is, in addition to making a decision about whether to move between industries, workers also make a decision about their formality status in an industry. The estimates yield a separate mobility cost for entering each possible industry for each formality status (table 4.6).[11] The results show it is always less costly to become formal while staying in the same industry than switching industries.

In both Mexico and Morocco, manufacturing appears to be a stepping stone to formal jobs because the switching cost is low (which implies that formal and informal workers perform similar roles or have similar skills). This result suggests that manufacturing is a key sector for formalizing the labor market. In Mexico, an average informal worker would find that the trade and other services sectors also have low costs of entering formal employment. In Morocco, restaurants and hotels have a low cost of transitioning from informality to formality. In urban Brazil, by contrast, commerce is the stepping stone for moving into formal jobs.

A worker changing employment status may have to deal with two potential sources of mobility friction: moving between industries, and moving between informal and formal employment. Three results are common for all three countries: (1) For an average informal worker, it is always less costly to become formal in the same industry than to switch industries. Industry-specific skill requirements might explain this finding. (2) The highest cost involves two sources of mobility friction: moving from informal to formal plus changing industries. This suggests that becoming formal adds to the cost of acquiring new industry-specific skills. For example, in each of the three countries, it is costly to become formal by moving from any sector into manufacturing. (3) The mobility cost is lowest when switching from formal to informal status within the same industry. In all

Table 4.6 Stepping-Stone Sectors to Formality: Labor Mobility Cost Estimates for Morocco, Mexico, and Brazil

From	To	Type	Agr/min	Manu	Commerce	Hotels	Services	Residual
Morocco								
Formal	Informal	Within	0.61	0.65	0.70	−0.11*	0.61	n.a.
Informal	Formal	Within	4.62	3.00	3.52	3.16	4.29	n.a.
Informal	Formal	Between	6.62	5.77	6.69	7.98	7.18	1.45
Formal	Formal	Between	3.22	2.51	2.78	5.60	4.34	1.91
Any	Informal	Between	2.57	3.32	3.49	4.85	3.33	n.a.
Mexico								
Formal	Informal	Within	1.00	1.06	1.13	0.47	0.69	n.a.
Informal	Formal	Within	3.09	2.97	3.17	3.22	2.92	n.a.
Informal	Formal	Between	5.78	4.90	4.70	6.04	4.89	1.29
Formal	Formal	Between	3.65	2.94	2.78	4.83	3.03	1.26
Any	Informal	Between	3.44	2.80	2.44	3.35	2.46	n.a.
Brazil								
Formal	Informal	Within	0.86	1.17	1.03	0.74	0.80	n.a.
Informal	Formal	Within	2.76	3.22	2.99	3.22	3.19	n.a.
Informal	Formal	Between	5.90	4.94	4.64	6.36	4.61	1.81
Formal	Formal	Between	3.66	2.67	2.58	4.92	2.88	1.02
Any	Informal	Between	4.19	2.98	2.77	3.89	2.55	n.a.

Source: Arias-Vázquez et al. 2013.
Note: Table 4.6 shows the estimated labor mobility cost as a ratio of the average annual wage of entering each industry (columns) for each formality status (rows). Agr/min = Agriculture/mining; Manu = Manufacturing; n.a. = not applicable.
* Not statistically different from zero.

countries, restaurants and hotels and other services have the lowest cost of switching from formal to informal. Institutional factors and labor market rigidities may be behind these similar results, producing similar mobility barriers to workers changing sectors and formality status.

Simulations of the dynamic effects of a trade-related shock for each country suggest that a reduction in domestic prices can lead to increased informal employment drawing from previously inactive or unemployed workers rather than through formal workers becoming informal. Some interesting results emerge about the paths of transition between formal, informal, and residual employment when removal of a tariff in the manufacturing sector lowers the domestic output price by 30 percent at time $t = 0$. As illustrated in figure 4.2, aggregate informal employment as a share of the working-age population increases smoothly after the tariff reduction. In Morocco, informal employment increases by 4 percentage points, from the original steady-state level of 38 percent of the labor force to the new steady-state level of 42 percent. In Mexico, the increase is 2 percentage points, from 36 to 38 percent. In Brazil, informal employment in the new equilibrium is 1 percentage point higher than in the initial steady state. Formal employment in all three countries remains fairly constant after the trade reform. Thus the majority of new informal workers comes from formerly inactive or unemployed workers who gradually enter the

Figure 4.2 Informal Employment Increases after a Positive Trade Shock because Previously Inactive Workers Enter the Labor Force

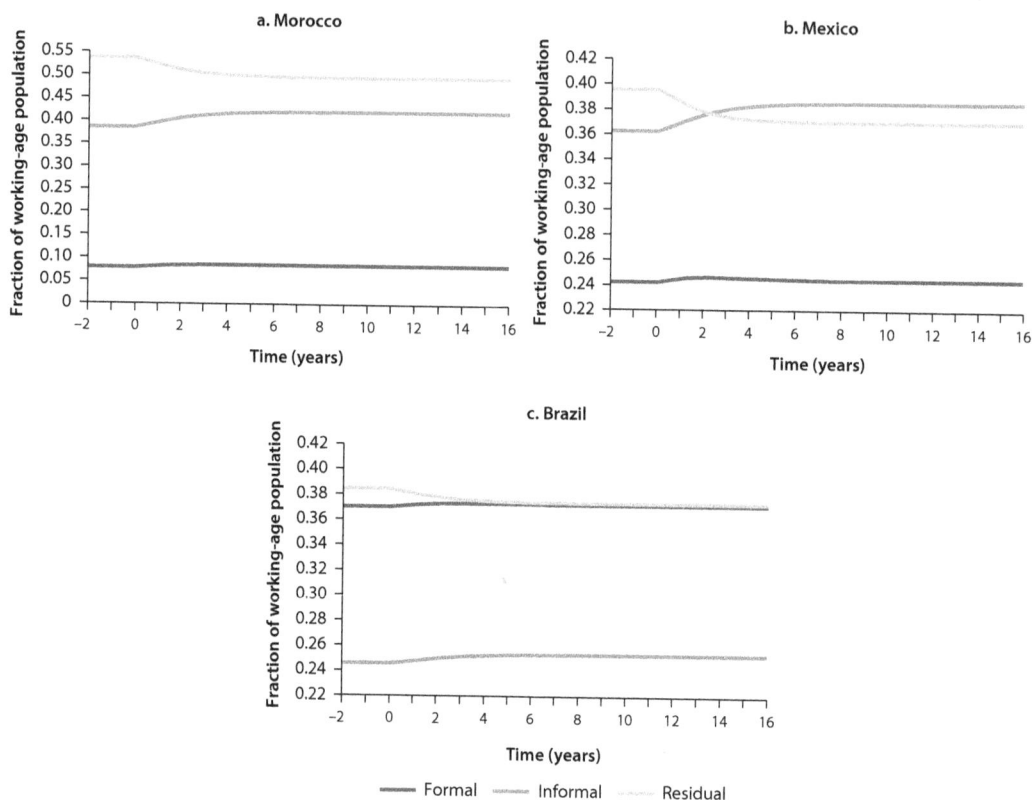

Source: Arias-Vázquez et al. 2013.
Note: Figure 4.2 shows simulations of the labor shares of the formal, informal, and residual sectors on the vertical axis for each time period on the horizontal axis, expressed in years, after removal of a tariff in the manufacturing sector lowers the domestic output price by 30 percent at time t = 0.

labor force. This result emerges because the costs of entry into formal employment are significantly higher than for entry into informal employment.

The simulation results for Morocco, Mexico, and Brazil are driven by the drop in manufacturing wages and the rise in real nonmanufacturing wages after trade liberalization, which spurs labor reallocation. For Morocco, the agriculture sector gains the most in labor share. In Mexico, the restaurants and hotels sector is unaffected by the trade reform, and commerce experiences only a marginal increase in labor share. In Brazil, agriculture and other services absorb most of the workers, whether entering from the residual sector or displaced from manufacturing. The differences between sectors are driven by differences in labor mobility costs.

The conclusion that increased informal employment is driven by workers entering from unemployment or inactivity rather than from formality is consistent with studies showing that informality increases due to lower formal job-finding rates rather than increases in formal job separations. Bosch,

Goni-Pacchioni, and Maloney (2012) used gross worker flows to measure the impact of trade liberalization on the rise of informality in Brazil and concluded that trade liberalization had only a small role in shaping informality trends in the 1990s, accounting for just 1–2.5 percent of the increase in informality, and that increases in informal employment stemmed from lower formal job-finding rates. This conclusion is also consistent with evidence from Mexico that the formal and informal sectors respond differently to economic downturns; Bosch and Maloney (2007) found that informality absorbs relatively more labor during downturns because the formal salaried sector stops creating new jobs but the informal sector does not.

Role of Firm Size: The Cases of Costa Rica and Morocco

Can workers find employment more easily in larger firms after a permanent trade-related shock, or do smaller firms offer more opportunities? This section explores how firm size affects mobility costs and labor-market dynamics after trade-related shocks in Costa Rica and Morocco. Using social security records, the analysis is extended to allow mobility costs to vary for formal workers entering firms of different sizes (small, medium, and large in terms of number of employees) within different industries.[12] In addition to the decision about whether to move between industries, the structural model of workers' sectoral employment choice incorporates a second decision, whether to enter a large-, small- or medium-sized firm within an industry. If labor mobility costs indeed vary by firm size, the estimation could have implications for how governments can best target policy responses to shocks. It appears, as will be seen, that labor-market dynamics after a trade shock are very country-specific.

When mobility costs are allowed to vary by size of the firm that workers enter, in some countries firm size does matter. The average mobility cost for workers entering different-sized firms was estimated for five separate industries, two traded and three nontraded, and the residual sector.[13] Figure 4.3 ranks industries and firms of different sizes according to the average cost of entering. For Costa Rica, the cost of entry depends more on industry than firm size, and the agriculture sector has the lowest entry costs for all firms. In Morocco, it is much easier to get a job in a large firm than in a small firm: in all sectors large firms have the lowest costs of entry.

This result has implications for where workers find employment after a permanent trade shock. Simulations using the toolkit disaggregated for firm size found that in Costa Rica and Morocco, agriculture firms, especially large ones, absorb the most reallocated labor. Figure 4.4 illustrates the results of the simulations of employment and wage responses to a 30 percent reduction in the price of manufacturing goods due to a permanent trade shock that occurs at time $t = 0$, comparing across industry and firm size.

The residual sector (unemployed and informal labor) is predicted to contract after the price shock, with workers most likely to enter agricultural employment. The higher real wage in all other sectors of the economy except manufacturing

Figure 4.3 Does Firm Size Affect Labor Mobility Costs in Costa Rica and Morocco?

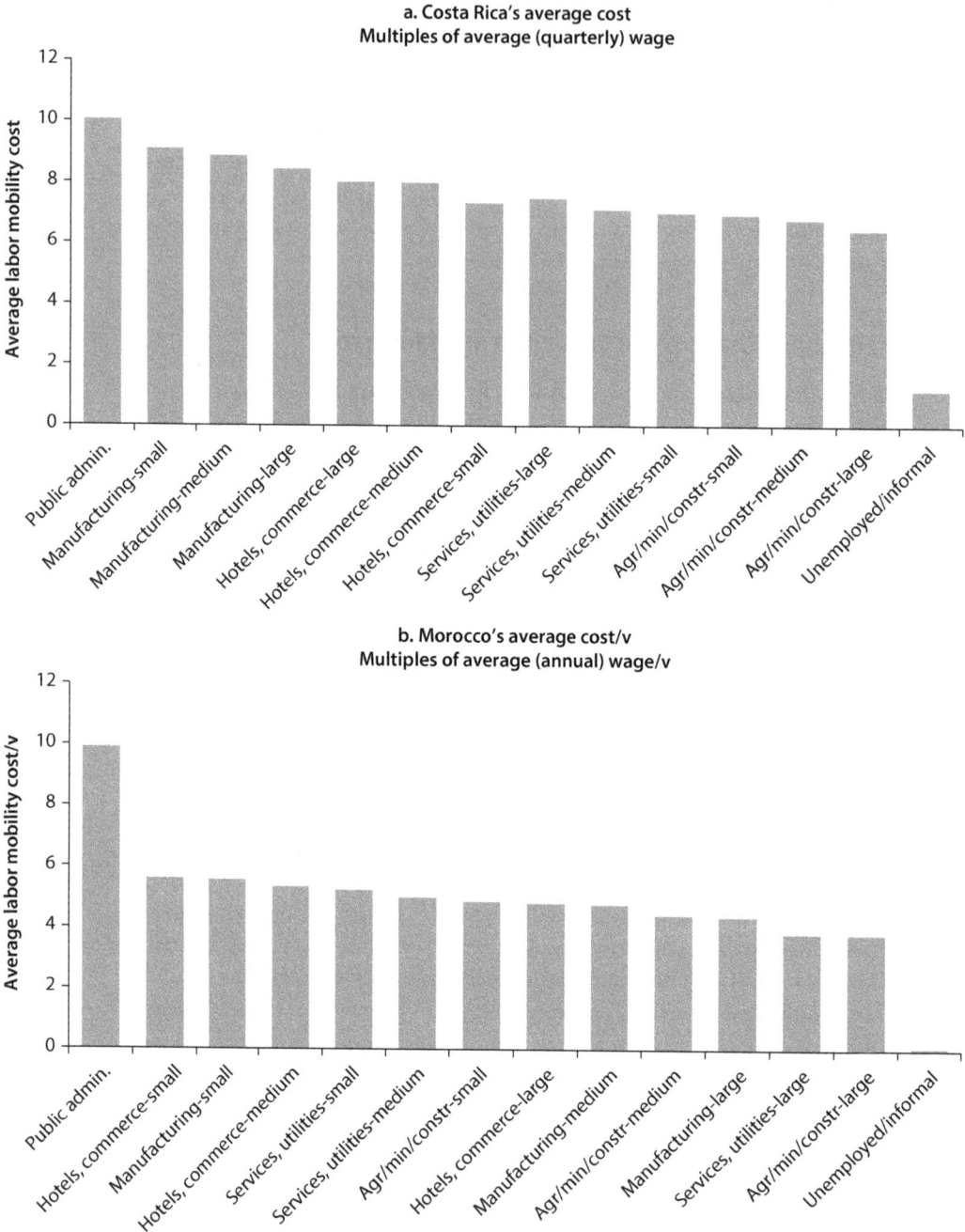

a. Costa Rica's average cost
Multiples of average (quarterly) wage

b. Morocco's average cost/v
Multiples of average (annual) wage/v

Note: Figure 4.3 presents labor mobility costs of entering different industries and firms of different size: small (30 employees or fewer), medium (31–100 employees), and large (more than 100 employees). Industry-firm size couplings are ranked according to the average mobility cost of entering. For Morocco, the framework is only able to identify the adjustment costs as a ratio of the variance of the welfare shocks, *C/v*. For Costa Rica, actual adjustment costs are identified. Agr/min/constr = Agriculture, forestry, fishing, mining, quarrying, construction.

increases the opportunity cost for unemployed individuals. Given the cost structure of the economy and the rational forward-looking behavior of workers, these workers choose to enter employment. However, employment is predicted to flow disproportionately into larger firms than small- and medium-sized firms because labor mobility costs are lower.

Figure 4.4 Wage and Employment Dynamics by Firm Size: The Post-Shock Employment Response in Large Firms Outweighs That in Small Firms

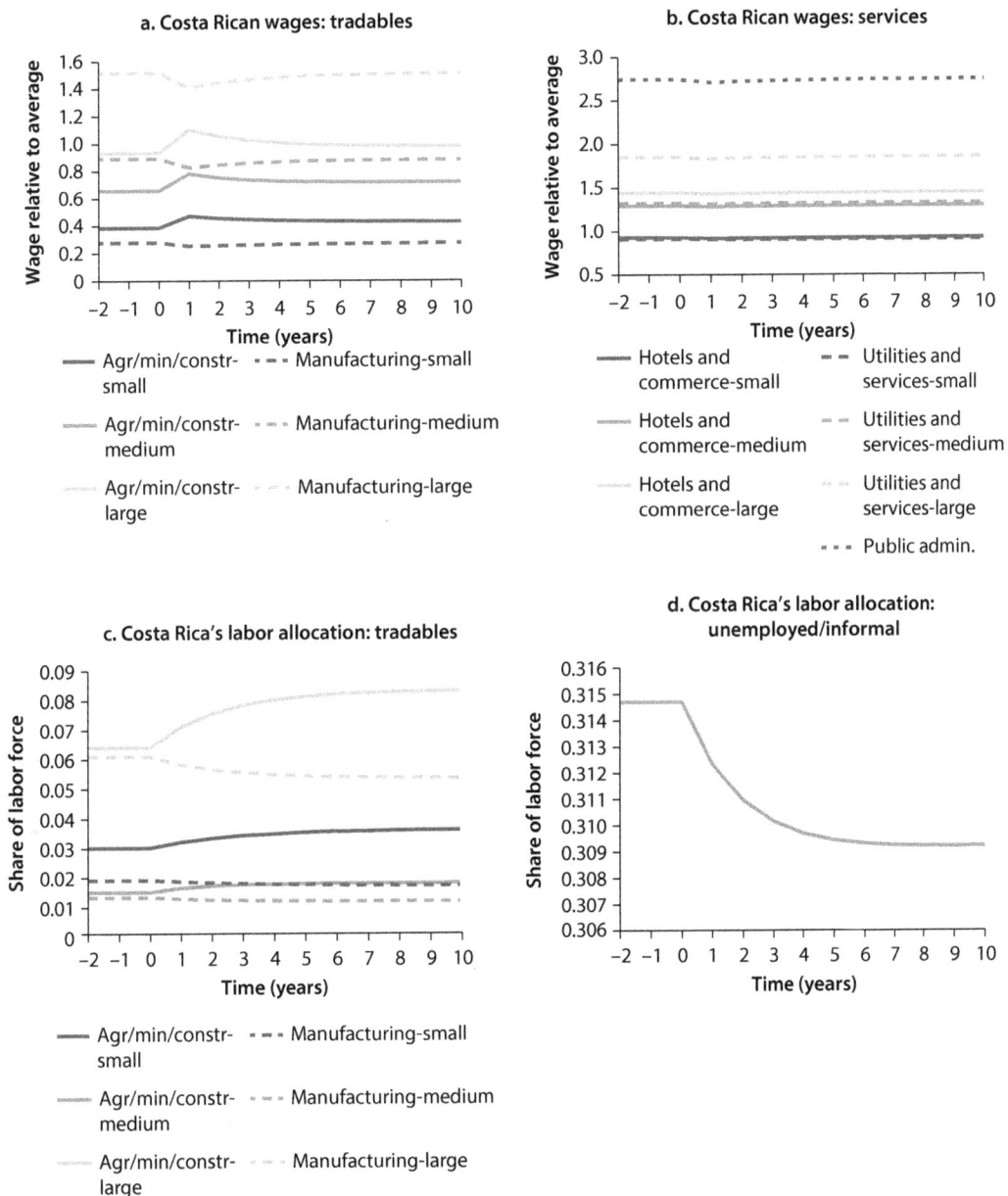

a. Costa Rican wages: tradables

b. Costa Rican wages: services

Agr/min/constr-small — Manufacturing-small

Agr/min/constr-medium — Manufacturing-medium

Agr/min/constr-large — Manufacturing-large

Hotels and commerce-small — Utilities and services-small

Hotels and commerce-medium — Utilities and services-medium

Hotels and commerce-large — Utilities and services-large

Public admin.

c. Costa Rica's labor allocation: tradables

d. Costa Rica's labor allocation: unemployed/informal

Agr/min/constr-small — Manufacturing-small

Agr/min/constr-medium — Manufacturing-medium

Agr/min/constr-large — Manufacturing-large

figure continues next page

Figure 4.4 **Wage and Employment Dynamics by Firm Size: The Post-Shock Employment Response in Large Firms Outweighs That in Small Firms** *(continued)*

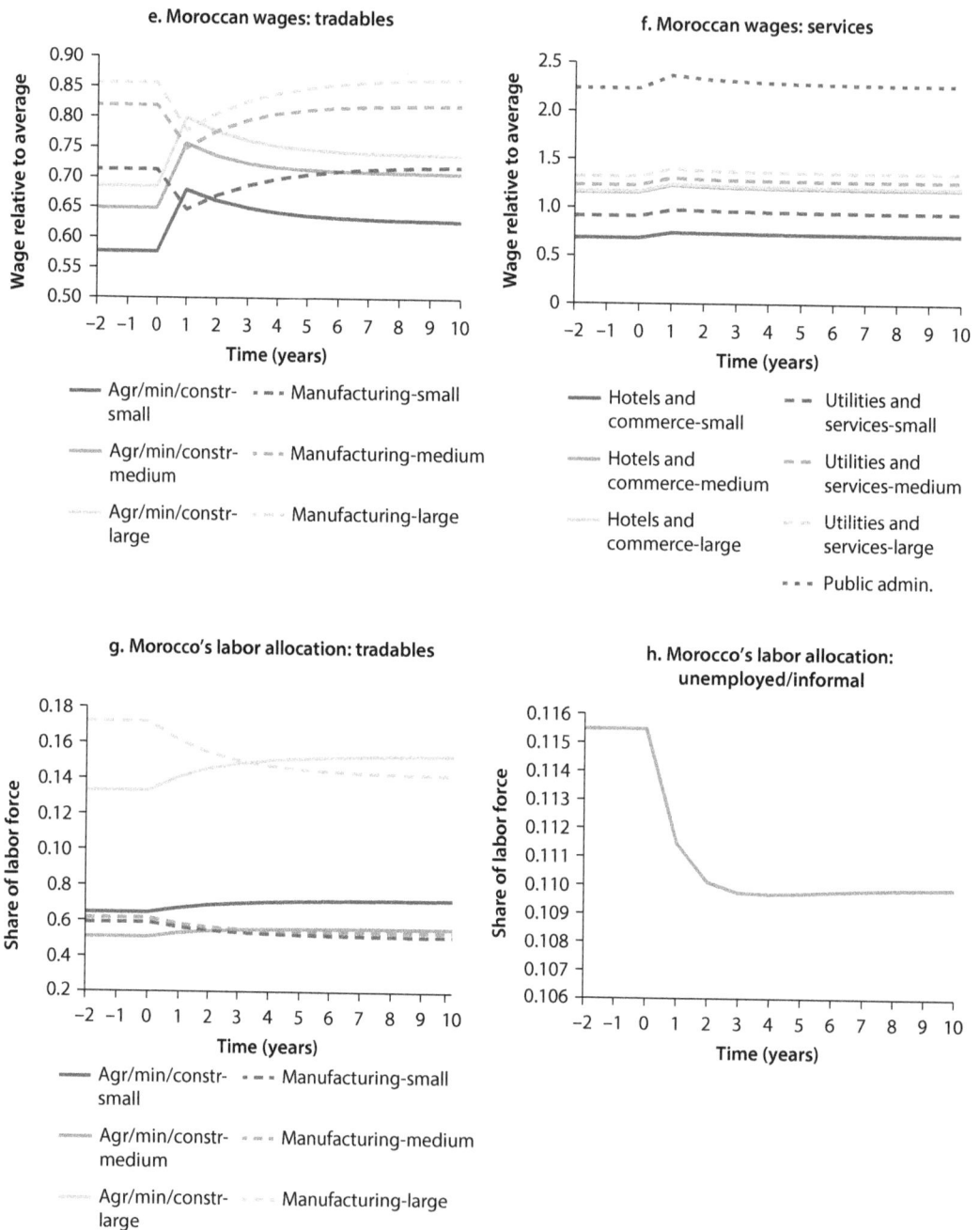

e. Moroccan wages: tradables

Legend:
— Agr/min/constr-small   - - - Manufacturing-small
— Agr/min/constr-medium   - - - Manufacturing-medium
— Agr/min/constr-large   - - - Manufacturing-large

f. Moroccan wages: services

Legend:
— Hotels and commerce-small   - - Utilities and services-small
— Hotels and commerce-medium   - - Utilities and services-medium
— Hotels and commerce-large   - - Utilities and services-large
- - - Public admin.

g. Morocco's labor allocation: tradables

Legend:
— Agr/min/constr-small   - - - Manufacturing-small
— Agr/min/constr-medium   - - - Manufacturing-medium
— Agr/min/constr-large   - - - Manufacturing-large

h. Morocco's labor allocation: unemployed/informal

Note: The graphs in figure 4.4 show simulations of labor market responses to a 30 percent decline in the price of output in the manufacturing sector due to a permanent trade shock that occurs at time $t = 0$. Wages relative to the average and share of the labor force, including the residual sector, for each sector are measured on the vertical axis, and time on the horizontal axis. The sector disaggregation is: agriculture, forestry, fishing, mining, quarrying, and construction; manufacturing; hotels, restaurants, and wholesale and retail trade; public administration; other services and utilities; and residual sector (unemployed, informal workers). Agr/min/constr = Agriculture, forestry, fishing, mining, quarrying, construction.

Notes

1. Firm-level data are used for capital adjustment cost parameters and household-level data for labor mobility cost parameters for the manufacturing and nonmanufacturing sectors, following a two-step estimation procedure similar to Artuç (2013). See appendix A for details of the estimation procedure and appendix B for details on the data.

2. The dynamic implications of a negative price shock are similar. There is a gradual, sluggish decline in capital. Real wages drop on impact and only partially recover, thus reaching a lower steady state. Employment declines gradually, as does output. It is noteworthy that the responsiveness of capital, wages, and employment to the size of a negative shock is actually opposite to the patterns observed for a positive shock: Aggregate capital becomes proportionately less responsive as the price shock becomes larger. The underlying cause is the depreciation rate; since it is costly to adjust capital and firms want to disinvest, it is convenient to let capital depreciate rather than pay the adjustment costs.

3. In other words, there is an interaction effect between the trade shock and the costs of adjusting capital. Capital adjustment costs create total and partial firm inaction. If the price shock arrives with a lower or no capital adjustment cost, firms that react will react much more quickly and sharply to a given shock, and some firms that were totally inactive before now respond to the shock. This occurs especially in the early years of the transition and only moderately in the long run.

4. To maximize the comparability of the Mexican results with the U.S. results in Artuç, Chaudhuri, and McLaren (2010), the same model, estimation methodology, and time period (1997–2005) are used, as is the same industry classification at the 1-digit classification level: agriculture and mining; construction; manufacturing; transportation and utilities; trade (wholesale and retail); and services (see also appendix B).

5. An alternative transition matrix for Mexico using household survey data that includes informal workers with comparable sector aggregation shows somewhat higher rates of transition into and out of manufacturing and commerce, but the trends are similar. By considering only between-sector worker transitions, both transition matrices understate the large within-sector transitions, including those between formality and informality, as observed in Maloney (1999).

6. The discount factor represents the degree to which the worker values the present over the future. The assumed value of the discount factor thus affects the worker's expected welfare, which is expressed as a present discounted value.

7. Fiess, Fugazza, and Maloney (2010) built these kinds of frictions into models of sectoral transitions and found that human capital accumulation is important to explaining the differing patterns of macroeconomic adjustment in high self-employment and low self-employment countries.

8. Although there is evidence of significant labor mobility between formal and informal sectors in Mexico, the results hold when the informal sector is excluded, although the estimates fall slightly.

9. Because the estimation strategy used to obtain the industry-specific labor mobility cost estimates follows Artuç (2013), they are not directly comparable to the industry-specific estimates from Artuç, Chaudhuri, and McLaren (2010).

10. This is illustrated in Kaplan, Lederman, and Robertson (2013), which used Mexican social security data to compare mobility costs for different levels of aggregation of industry classifications. Going from the 1-digit level (seven separate industries) to the 4-digit level (271 separate industries) increases mobility cost estimates by at least a factor of 10.

11. Industries are aggregated into five sectors: agriculture, mining, construction and utilities; manufacturing; commerce; hotels and restaurants; and other services. Each sector is subdivided between formal and informal. A worker who receives social security benefits is considered formal. There is also a residual sector that captures individuals who are either unemployed or out of the labor force.

12. The three categories of firm size analyzed are small (30 employees or fewer), medium (31–100), and large (more than 100). Informal and unemployed workers are combined into a residual sector. See appendix B for details.

13. The industries were agriculture, forestry, fishing, mining, quarrying, and construction; manufacturing; hotels, restaurants, and wholesale and retail trade; public administration; and other services and utilities.

References

Arias-Vázquez, F. J., E. Artuç, D. Lederman, and D. Rojas. 2013. "Trade, Informal Employment and Labor Adjustment Costs." Policy Research Working Paper 6614, World Bank, Washington, DC.

Artuç, E. 2013. "Estimating Dynamic Discrete Choice Models with Unspecified Aggregate Shocks." Policy Research Working Paper 6480, World Bank, Washington, DC.

Artuç, E., G. Bet, I. Brambilla, and G. Porto. 2013. "Trade Shocks, Firm-Level Investment Inaction, and Labor Market Responses." Unpublished manuscript, International Trade Department, Poverty Reduction and Economic Management, World Bank, Washington, DC.

Artuç, E., S. Chaudhuri, and J. McLaren. 2008. "Delay and Dynamics in Labor Market Adjustment: Simulation Results." *Journal of International Economics* 75 (1): 1–13.

———. 2010. "Trade Shocks and Labor Adjustment: A Structural Empirical Approach." *American Economic Review* 100: 1008–45.

Bosch, M., E. Goni-Pacchioni, and W. Maloney 2012. "Trade Liberalization, Labor Reforms and Formal-Informal Employment Dynamics." *Labour Economics* 19: 653–67.

Bosch, M., and W. Maloney. 2007. "Gross Worker Flows in the Presence of Informal Labor Markets: Evidence from Mexico, 1987–2002." IZA Discussion Paper Series 2864, Institute for the Study of Labor, Bonn, Germany.

Cooper, R. W., and J. C. Haltiwanger. 2006. "On the Nature of Capital Adjustment Costs." *Review of Economic Studies* 73 (3): 611–33.

Evans, D., and B. Jovanovic. 1989. "An Estimated Model of Entrepreneurial Choice under Liquidity Constraints." *Journal of Political Economy* 97: 808–27.

Fajnzylber, P., W. Maloney, and G. Montes Rojas. 2006. "Microenterprise Dynamics in Developing Countries: How Similar Are They to Those in the Industrialized World? Evidence from Mexico." *World Bank Economic Review* 29 (3): 389–419.

Fiess, N., M. Fugazza, and W. Maloney. 2010. "Informal Self-Employment and Macroeconomic Fluctuations." *Journal of Development Economics* 91 (2): 211–26.

Kaplan, D. S., D. Lederman, and R. Robertson. 2013. "Worker-Level Adjustment Costs in a Developing Country: Evidence from Mexico." Unpublished manuscript, International Trade Department, Poverty Reduction and Economic Management, World Bank, Washington, DC.

Maloney, W. 1999. "Does Informality Imply Segmentation in Urban Labor Markets? Evidence from Sectoral Transitions in Mexico." *World Bank Economic Review* 13 (2): 275–302.

Robertson, R., and D. H. Dutkowsky. 2002. "Labor Adjustment Costs in a Destination Country: The Case of Mexico." *Journal of Development Economics* 67: 29–54.

World Bank. 2012. *Jobs: World Development Report 2013.* Washington, DC: International Bank for Reconstruction and Development/World Bank.

CHAPTER 5

Labor Market Effects of Shocks: Validating Simulations with Regression Analysis

Abstract

Simple econometric models are used to quantify the role of mobility costs in shaping labor market adjustment to structural trade shocks. Unlike the complex structural models previously discussed, the analyses presented here do not make any assumptions about how labor markets function. In other words, the data are allowed to speak for themselves.

Structural economic reforms are found to lead to positive outcomes for employment and wages, in contrast to the common perception that structural reforms destroy jobs. And no conclusive evidence was found that structural reforms increase equilibrium unemployment, which suggests that the increase in employment stems from increases in informal employment, which is consistent with the findings of the structural models.

Using micro-level data on Mexican workers, the impact of different types of job separation on worker welfare was tested. For workers displaced due to a plant closing, a likely outcome after a trade-related shock, it can take a long time for wages to recover—longer than for other separated workers. These workers also suffer longer spells of unemployment, but after reentering work they are just as likely as other separated workers to be employed in the formal sector.

This chapter explores the role of mobility costs in shaping labor adjustment to structural trade shocks without imposing assumptions about how labor markets function. "Reduced-form" econometric regression models are used to analyze the equilibrium effects of a trade policy reform on the labor market. This makes it possible to test the predictions of the structural choice models of the toolkit discussed in chapters 3 and 4. Reduced-form regressions offer a complementary approach to analyzing the effects of structural reforms, such as trade reforms, on labor markets in developing countries, the results of which might inform policy decisions. The toolkit methodologies used in previous chapters yield structural empirical analyses that estimate mobility costs, which are then used to simulate labor adjustment patterns across countries, industries, and types of firm. Although very rich, the structural empirical approach relies on relatively stringent theoretical assumptions.

Using a variety of datasets, it was possible to validate previous simulation results with observed adjustment costs in terms of the sluggish response of labor to trade-related shocks. This is done through two empirical analyses commissioned for this report. The first examines in a large cross-country sample a comprehensive set of macro-level labor market outcomes that may be driven by structural reforms. Among the outcomes are unemployment, total employment, female employment, wages, and labor force participation. The second analysis explores labor adjustment at the micro level by measuring determinants of post-reform labor force status in Mexico, where worker reallocation stems from reform-induced plant closures.

Macroeconomic Analysis: Impact of Structural Reforms on Labor Outcomes

How do country labor markets respond to trade and other structural reforms that are comprehensive rather than sector specific? Based on Hollweg, Lederman, and Mitra (2012), the analysis first looks at whether labor market trends change after reforms by comparing the cross-country average of each of the outcome variables relative to the year of reform. A more rigorous instrumental variable approach is then applied to suggest causal effects of reforms on labor market outcomes.

Both approaches show that structural reforms lead to positive outcomes for workers at the macroeconomic level. There seems to be substantial evidence that structural reforms were associated with ex post increases in employment, despite higher average unemployment levels. Because the regressions control for the labor force participation of formal workers, the increase stems from informal workers. Wages also take an upward turn after economic reforms. This increase in wages and its effects on the incentives for workers to join the labor market are consistent with the results of the simulation-based microeconomic analysis in chapter 4, particularly the analysis of informality. Although it is not possible from the data to determine whether increased employment is driven by a substitution effect (a higher opportunity cost of leisure) or an income effect (added workers to offset household income losses), after a reduction in tariffs, economy-wide real wages rise, providing incentives for workers to enter the formal labor force by moving out of informality.

Previous studies have found that countries that are more open to trade have lower unemployment. Two important cross-country studies—by Dutt, Mitra, and Ranjan (2009) and Felbermayr, Prat, and Schmerer (2011)—show that countries with less protectionist trade policies have lower unemployment, even after controlling for other policies and institutions that have more direct impact on labor markets. Dutt, Mitra, and Ranjan (2009) also found that in the short run trade reforms are associated with higher unemployment but are followed in the long run by a reduction to a lower equilibrium unemployment rate. Wacziarg and Wallack (2004) studied the impact of 25 liberalization episodes on labor reallocation across sectors; using the Sachs and Warner (1995) criteria to define these episodes, they found only weak evidence that liberalization had negative effects on industry employment shares.

This analysis differs from previous studies in identifying the impact for the 10-year periods before and after the year of reform. While this approach can limit the number of observations, it yields greater confidence in the impact of structural reforms on labor market outcomes for countries studied. For each country, the analysis covers a maximum of 10 years before the structural reform and 10 years after. It covers the same sample of countries and country structural reform dates as Wacziarg and Welch (2008), where the reform date is the date after which all Sachs-Warner openness criteria are met continuously.[1] Wacziarg and Welch (2008) updated the Sachs-Warner 1995 dates of reform through 2001. The resulting sample consists of 88 countries, both developed and developing (see appendix B).

Even though the approach is reduced form, economic theory and intuition should still guide the econometric specification. For example, trade theory suggests it is necessary to control for the labor force participation rate when considering the impact of trade liberalization on other labor market outcomes. In a Ricardian model of trade with search frictions, wages will increase in the long run due to trade liberalization.[2] For a given labor force participation rate, this will lower the unemployment rate. The increase in wages will also create incentives for workers to look for jobs and lead to higher labor force participation. Real GDP and working-age population are used as additional control variables. To the extent that these variables are growing over time, they may also affect labor market outcomes beyond those stemming from trade reforms.

The analysis first looks at the cross-country average of each of the labor market variables relative to the reform year to see if labor market trends change after liberalization. Each labor market outcome variable is regressed on dummy variables for each year on either side of the reform (see appendix A for details of the specification used). The coefficient of each dummy variable represents the cross-country average of the labor-market variable in its corresponding time period relative to the level in the year of reform, and is plotted in figure 5.1.[3] All of the a panels in figure 5.1 show results with no variables in the estimation other than country fixed effects; additional variables are controlled for in the b panels, including the labor force participation rate, real GDP, and the working-age population. The labor force participation rate is defined here to exclude informal workers, which affects interpretation of the results relating to employment and labor force participation.

Post-reform average labor market outcomes look strikingly different from pre-reform trends, with wages and employment in particular rising after reforms. On average, unemployment rates are higher after reform than before, both with and without significant variance in the average. However, employment levels are also higher on average after the reform, with and without

Figure 5.1 Average Labor Market Trends Pre- and Post-Reform: Employment and Wage Effects Are Especially Positive

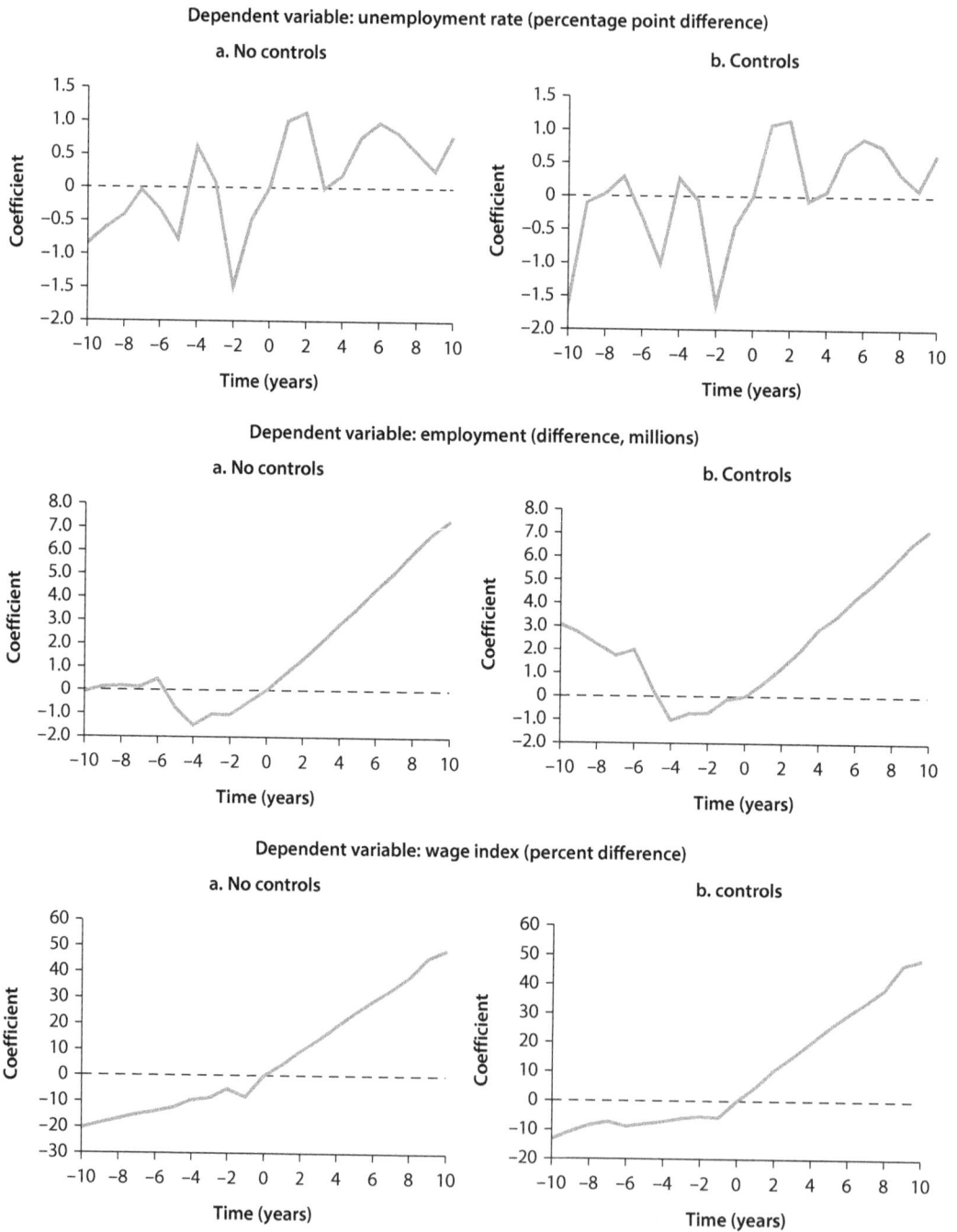

Dependent variable: unemployment rate (percentage point difference)

a. No controls

b. Controls

Dependent variable: employment (difference, millions)

a. No controls

b. Controls

Dependent variable: wage index (percent difference)

a. No controls

b. controls

figure continues next page

Figure 5.1 Average Labor Market Trends Pre- and Post-Reform: Employment and Wage Effects Are Especially Positive (continued)

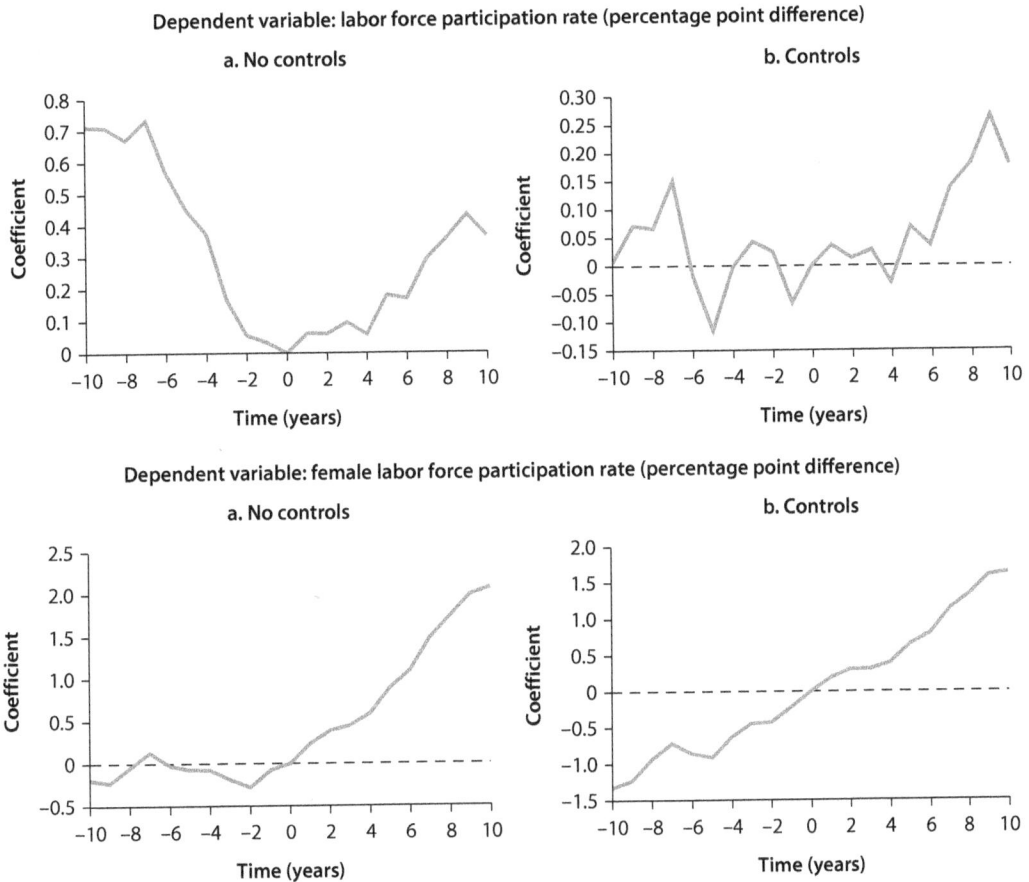

Dependent variable: labor force participation rate (percentage point difference)

a. No controls

b. Controls

Dependent variable: female labor force participation rate (percentage point difference)

a. No controls

b. Controls

Source: Hollweg, Lederman, and Mitra 2012.
Note: Each graph in figure 5.1 plots the cross-country average for each labor market outcome variable relative to its level in the reform year on the vertical axis against time plotted on the horizontal axis (time = 0 in the year of reform). Each labor market outcome variable is regressed on dummy variables for each year up to 10 years on either side of the reform. Controls in the B panels include real GDP, working-age population, and labor force participation (except for the regression in which labor force participation is the dependent variable).

controls, rising consistently and relatively steeply. In the case of the wage index, the rising trend observed before reform becomes steeper after reform. Labor force participation rates, both overall and female, are also relatively steeper post-reform. However, the results look significantly different with the controls than without. While the overall labor force participation rate declines before the reform, after controls are in place this trend disappears. The opposite is true for the female participation rate. This highlights the need for care when choosing the empirical specification because it will affect policy interpretation of the results.

It is important to distinguish between correlation and causation, because the relationship between labor market outcomes and the reform year is likely to be endogenous. The previous exercise documents the empirical regularity stemming from correlations in the data, but it is not a statement of causation. The likely endogeneity means that the adoption and timing of reforms can depend on multiple economic and political factors and the interactions between them. It is well known that macroeconomic policies and conditions themselves determine structural reforms. For example, poor macroeconomic performance and conditions (which might include high unemployment or high inflation) could lead governments to seek technical help from multilateral institutions and undertake extensive structural reforms (as with IMF-type programs). Thus reforms could be endogenous to unemployment rates and other labor market outcomes. Nevertheless, these empirical regularities are hard to ignore, highlighting the need for more rigorous analysis of the relationship between structural reforms and labor market outcomes by correcting for potential endogeneity.

The endogeneity problem is tackled using instrumental variable regressions to identify a causal effect. Each labor market outcome variable is regressed on a time trend, the square of the time trend, the set of control variables described previously, and an endogenous reform dummy variable that takes a value of 1 every year after the reform (see appendix A for details). Variables are selected to instrument the endogenous reform dummy variable.

The instruments are based on the theoretical literature on the political economy of reforms. Hollweg, Lederman, and Mitra (2012) drew on this literature to identify a fairly extensive list of instrumental variables for the structural reform dummy.[4]

- The *external debt-to-GDP ratio* can be a good instrument for reforms because, while it triggers reforms (for example, through conditional IMF assistance), it does not by itself affect unemployment. Rather, it is government spending and the budget deficit that are related to unemployment and other labor market outcomes.
- Another factor that could affect the likelihood of reform is a country's *terms of trade*. If the import price falls and terms of trade improve, the proportion of voters supporting reform will increase. In addition, prior to the economic reforms implemented by many developing countries late in the twentieth century, most developing countries were so closed that their external terms of trade would not have affected their labor market outcomes.
- Increases in democratization make it harder for protectionist governments to maintain political support in developing countries and the *five-year change in a country's democracy score* is a valid instrument because it enhances the probability of trade liberalization.
- "Status quo bias"—the lack of support for reforms because of uncertainty about the winners and losers from reforms—explains why the *one-year lagged endogenous dummy variable* is a valid instrument. Once reform occurs and winners and losers are revealed, the reforms will continue to be supported. That is, once an economy is reformed, the likelihood of reversal is low. Therefore, whether or not the economy was in a state of reform in the previous period will determine the current state.

Taken together, the instrumenting approach concludes that structural reforms lead to positive outcomes for employment, and by affecting relative prices structural reforms create redistribution effects in favor of workers through higher wages. This conclusion is in sharp contrast to the widely held perception that structural reforms destroy jobs. Because of controls for the time trend and real GDP, the results show the impact of structural reforms on labor-market outcomes beyond what happens through their impact on growth. Even when the time trend is highly significant and positive, there is solid evidence that structural reforms have a positive effect on employment and the wage index.

Evidence of a causal effect of reforms on unemployment rates is inconclusive, however, even though on average unemployment rates are higher after reforms. The conclusion is therefore that the increase in employment is driven by an increase in informal employment, because the regressions control for the labor force participation rate of formal workers. The regression evidence on the effect of structural reforms on formal participation rates (overall and female) is somewhat inconclusive despite a positive time trend and a positive effect of real GDP; to the extent that structural reforms spur economic growth, women participate more in the work force.

Microeconomic Analysis: Job Displacement and Reallocation in Mexico

How do labor markets reabsorb workers displaced through no fault of their own? This portion of the analysis, based on Arias-Vázquez and Lederman (2013), uses micro-level regression analysis to estimate the post-shock welfare of Mexican workers who lose their jobs because of plant closings (one potential outcome of trade shocks). The results can inform labor policies by identifying the impact of job displacement.

Destruction and creation of jobs are fundamental to efficient allocation of resources, but how labor markets reabsorb displaced workers is an important question. For example, exporting industries tend to grow with a lag but import-competing firms tend to contract or exit rapidly during periods of trade reform or other permanent trade-related shocks. The uncoordinated death of import-competing firms and the birth and expansion of exporting firms might cause spells of unemployment to be different for workers displaced due to a trade-related shock than for other workers in the economy.

An important contribution of this analysis to the literature is the ability to identify the cause of job separation. A reduced-form approach to studying the effects of job displacement on labor market outcomes was applied by Jacobson, LaLonde, and Sullivan (1993); Kaplan, Martinez, and Robertson (2005); Couch and Placzek (2010); Davis and Haltiwanger (1992); and Ruhm (1991a, 1991b), among others. Studying changes in formal-sector wages after job separation in Mexico, Kaplan, Martinez, and Robertson (2005) found large wage losses in regions with less economic activity and in periods of high unemployment. A limitation of that study is that the authors could not identify the cause of job separation (voluntary, plant closing, etc.). Arias-Vázquez and Lederman (2013), by contrast, were able to distinguish episodes of job separation that are random from those that are non-random (i.e., workers who are fired or who quit), which allowed them to use reduced-form regressions to determine the role of mobility costs in labor market adjustments for displaced workers.

Although the analysis focuses on workers displaced by plant closings, it also considers labor outcomes for workers who left jobs for three other reasons. The analysis uses Mexican Labor Force Survey data to identify four mutually exclusive causes of employment separation: quitting, involuntary separation (being fired), employers and self-employed who closed their own business, and displacement due to plant closure. Post-separation labor market outcomes are also collected for these individual workers, including wages, formality status, hours of work, job tenure, and a range of demographic characteristics. The inclusion of informal employment is crucial, since informal workers account for more than half of Mexico's total employment.

There are marked differences in the labor market outcomes of individuals displaced by a plant closing and those who experienced other types of job separation (table 5.1). Among the four sources of job separation, workers who experienced a plant closing were most likely to be employed post-shock, and least likely to be out of the labor force. Workers who were fired were most likely to be unemployed.

The effects of random job displacement on current labor market outcomes are explored from three angles; the reduced-form approach allows a different empirical specification to be used for each. Because job displacement appears to affect workers randomly, it can be argued that the estimated effects are causal rather than due to worker characteristics. By focusing on random displacement events, it is possible to capture the costs of mobility arising from labor market frictions rather than from observable or unobservable worker characteristics.

1. Reduced-form regressions are used to make an average comparison between the benchmark category of workers in the non-separated group and those who experienced each type of job separation for each labor market outcome.

Table 5.1 Labor Market Outcomes Vary by Job Separation Type

	Current labor force status		
	Employed	Unemployed	Out of labor force
Type of Separation			
Plant closing	71.7	9.9	18.4
Discharged/fired	61.4	14.2	24.4
Quit	42.5	4.1	53.5
Closed own business	44.4	5.1	50.5

Source: Arias-Vázquez and Lederman 2013.
Note: Table 5.1 shows the percentage of the population that was employed, unemployed, or out of the labor force at the time of the labor force survey (in each column) for workers that have in the past experienced each type of job separation (in each row).

2. Adding lagged indicators into the regression investigates whether the impact of job displacement on labor outcomes persists over a 10-year period. For example, the impacts of a job displacement that occurred seven years ago on current outcomes might differ from those of a displacement that occurred only one or two years ago.
3. A third estimation strategy identifies the impact of the type of job separation and other covariates on the duration of unemployment after job separation (see appendix A for a formal presentation of the empirical models and estimation strategies).

Although a job displacement does not permanently reduce real wages, it can take several years for wages to recover fully. Wages are initially 11 percent lower for workers displaced by a plant closing than those of nondisplaced workers in the first two years after displacement. Panel a of figure 5.2 illustrates the magnitude and duration of the impact of a plant closing on the real wages of a displaced worker compared to a nondisplaced worker. The wage gap narrows to 6 percent after the fourth year following the plant closing, and wages recover completely after nine years.

A displacement event does not, however, negatively affect the probability of a worker finding a formal job. Displaced and nondisplaced workers are equally likely to be formally employed. The probability of (re)entering the formal sector after job displacement is negatively affected only in the short run, as illustrated in panel b of figure 5.2. Although displaced workers are 10 percent less likely to (re)enter the formal sector within the same year as a plant closing, they recover

Figure 5.2 Plant Closings in Mexico Have a Persistent Negative Impact on Real Wages but Not on Formality Status

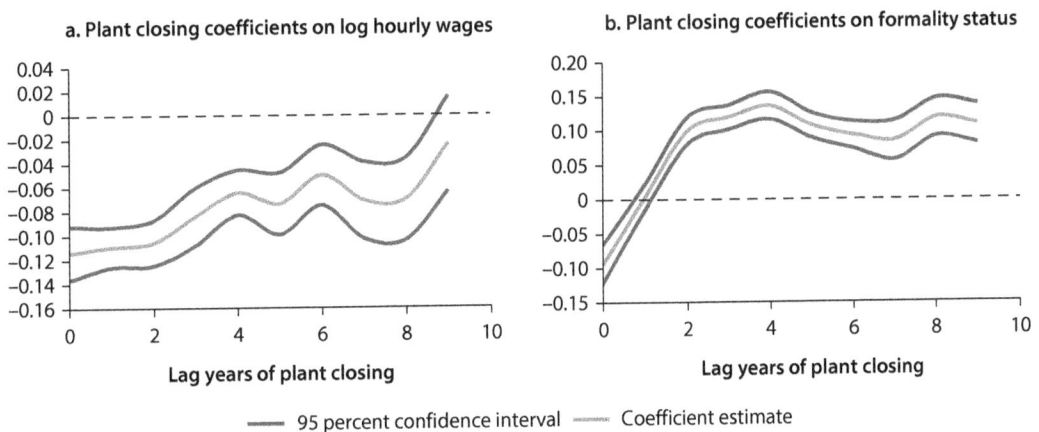

a. Plant closing coefficients on log hourly wages

b. Plant closing coefficients on formality status

Lag years of plant closing

Lag years of plant closing

——— 95 percent confidence interval ——— Coefficient estimate

Source: Arias-Vázquez and Lederman 2013.
Note: Panel a of figure 5.2 plots the percentage difference between the wages of a displaced worker and a nondisplaced worker (which is the estimated coefficient on the lagged displacement variable) on the vertical axis against each year since job displacement on the horizontal axis (where 0 is the year of the plant closing). Panel b plots the percentage difference in the probability of being employed in the formal sector for a displaced compared to a nondisplaced worker. All regressions control for years of education, gender, marital status, age, age squared, state, survey period, and industry fixed effects.

rapidly from this negative shock. A full year after plant closure, both displaced and nondisplaced workers have the same probability of formal employment.

The type of job separation and a worker's gender matter for the length of unemployment and for labor force exit. Workers displaced by a plant closing experience longer periods of unemployment than other types of separated workers (figure 5.3, panel a). In Mexico, the period of unemployment ends in about 12 months, and men displaced by plant closure are likely to find employment faster than women (figure 5.3, panel b).

Taken together, the results indicate that displaced workers incur significant adjustment costs. Most of the adjustment costs are borne by workers in the form of lower wages that take a long time to recover to the levels in their previous jobs. This includes workers accepting alternative employment with lower wages and those with temporary periods of unemployment. The length of the adjustment depends on the type of separation and on average exceeds 9 years for workers displaced because of plant closure. Moreover, the adjustment costs are not borne through informality. This conclusion, consistent with the findings of chapter 4, implies that increases in informality arising from trade reforms are due to new workers entering the labor market rather than reallocation of displaced workers. Thus the empirical results of the reduced-form approach validate the predictions of the structural modeling approach discussed earlier.

Figure 5.3 Unemployment after a Plant Closure Is Longer than for Other Types of Job Separation, Especially for Women

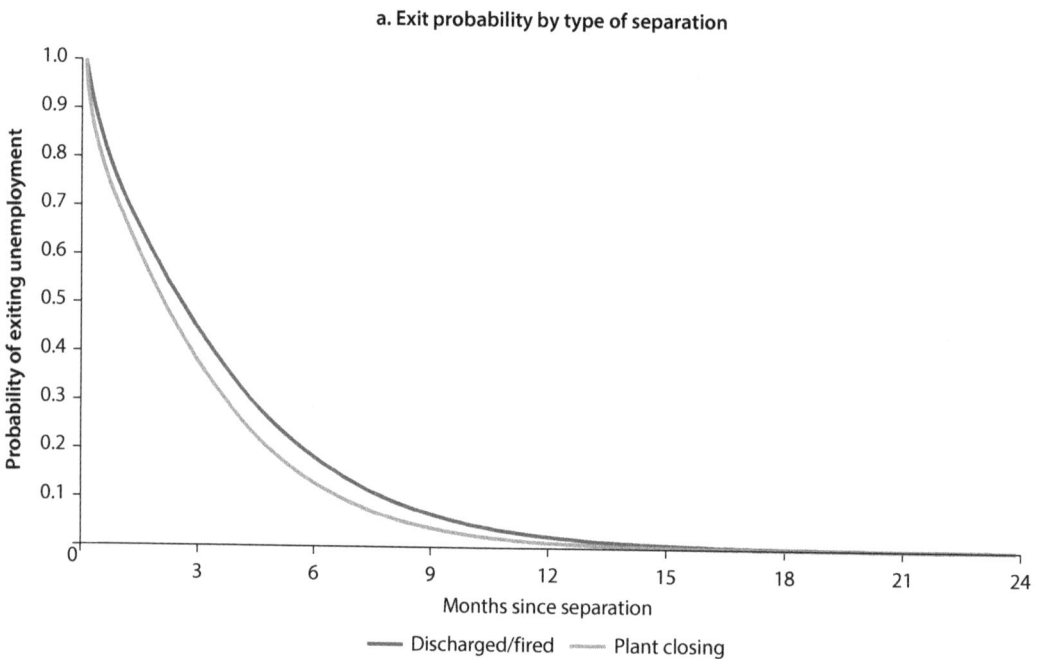

a. Exit probability by type of separation

figure continues next page

Figure 5.3 Unemployment after a Plant Closure Is Longer than for Other Types of Job Separation, Especially for Women *(continued)*

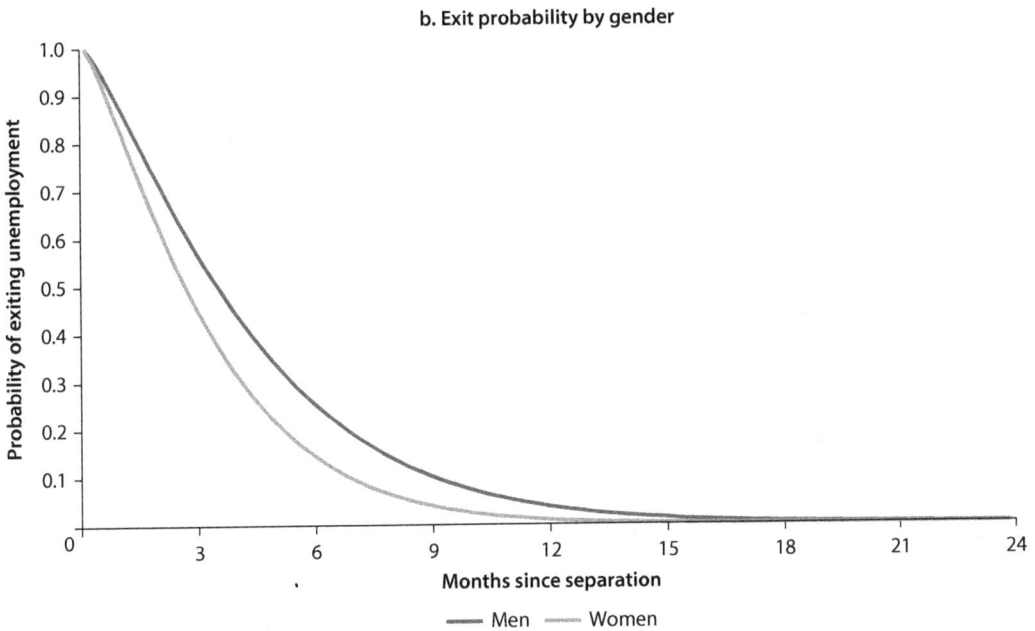

b. Exit probability by gender

Source: Arias-Vázquez and Lederman 2013.
Note: Figure 5.3 plots the probability of exiting unemployment on the vertical axis against each month since job displacement on the horizontal axis (where 0 is the month of displacement). The exit probabilities are compared for workers displaced due to plant closure to those who were fired in Panel a, and for men and women displaced due to plant closure in Panel b.

These results highlight the need for policies to be carefully tailored when permanent trade-related shocks are addressed. If trade liberalization is likely to lead to plant closures as industries adjust, it is noteworthy that workers displaced through no fault of their own will be affected for long periods after job separation. This outcome has implications for the types of support programs that aim to ease worker adjustment to employment or income shocks, including trade-related shocks. Policy implications are discussed in chapter 6.

Notes

1. Sachs and Warner (1995) classified a country as open if it does not display any of the following characteristics: (1) average tariff rates of 40 percent of more; (2) nontariff barriers covering 40 percent or more of trade; (3) a black market exchange rate at least 20 percent lower than the official exchange rate; (4) a state monopoly on major exports; or (5) a socialist economic system.

2. The long-run impact of trade liberalization is a lower unemployment rate, and increases in employment, the labor force participation rate, and the wage rate. The movement from autarky to trade will raise the price of an exportable good and the wage rate in that sector. Thus, wages will increase due to trade liberalization.

3. For some countries and years in the sample, labor market data may be interpolated using GDP growth between labor force survey years. It is not possible to correct this limitation, and this would affect the time series of these variables. However, the regression coefficients are based on a cross-sectional panel of countries 10 years pre- and post-reform, and thus this limitation is not likely to significantly influence the results.

4. A valid instrument is one that is correlated with the endogenous regressor yet orthogonal to the errors. Hollweg, Lederman, and Mitra (2012) performed three empirical tests of instrument validity: (1) To assess how well instruments correlate with the endogenous regressor, it is sufficient to examine the significance of the excluded instruments using the R-squared of the first stage regression, referred to as the partial-R2 (Shea 1997). (2) The Kleibergen Paap F-statistic is reported to test for weak instruments. (3) Whether the instruments are orthogonal to the errors can be tested in an over-identified model where the number of instruments is greater than the number of endogenous regressors using the Hansen J-statistic. In many of the specifications considered, the instruments exhibit the desired characteristics: a fair degree of correlation with the instrumented variable and joint orthogonality of the instruments with respect to the error term. The fixed-effects regressions also control for unobservable country characteristics and the time trend and its quadratic control for unobserved labor market outcomes that are trending over time, further reducing the likelihood of omitted variables. However, if there are omitted variables that are correlated with the labor market outcomes beyond their effect through the instrumental variables, the instruments would not be orthogonal to the error term, and the causal interpretation would be invalidated.

References

Arias-Vázquez, F. J., and D. Lederman. 2013. "Displaced Workers and Labor Market Outcomes: Evidence from Mexico." Unpublished manuscript, International Trade Department, Poverty Reduction and Economic Management, World Bank, Washington, DC.

Couch, K., and D. Placzek. 2010. "Earnings Losses of Displaced Workers Revisited." *American Economic Review* 100 (1): 572–89.

Davis, S. J., and J. C. Haltiwanger. 1992. "Gross Job Creation, Gross Job Destruction, and Employment Reallocation." *Quarterly Journal of Economics* 107 (3): 819–63.

Dutt, P., D. Mitra, and P. Ranjan. 2009. "International Trade and Unemployment: Theory and Cross-National Evidence." *Journal of International Economics* 78 (1): 32–44.

Felbermayr, G., J. Prat, and H. Schmerer. 2011. "Trade and Unemployment: What Do the Data Say?" *European Economic Review* 55 (6): 741–58.

Hollweg, C. H., D. Lederman, and D. Mitra. 2012. "Structural Reforms and Labor-Market Outcomes: International Panel Data Evidence." Unpublished manuscript, International Trade Department, Poverty Reduction and Economic Management, World Bank, Washington, DC.

Jacobson, L. S., R. J. LaLonde, and D. G. Sullivan. 1993. "Earnings Losses of Displaced Workers." *American Economic Review* 83 (4): 685–709.

Kaplan, D., G. Martinez, and R. Robertson. 2005. "What Happens to Wages after Displacement?" *Economia: Journal of the Latin American and Caribbean Economic Association* 5 (2): 197–234.

Ruhm, C. J. 1991a. "Are Workers Permanently Scarred by Job Displacements?" *American Economic Review* 81 (1): 319–24.

———. 1991b. "Displacement Induced Joblessness." *Review of Economics and Statistics* 73 (3): 517–22.

Sachs, J., and A. Warner. 1995. "Economic Reforms and the Process of Global Integration." *Brookings Papers on Economic Activity* 1: 1–118.

Shea, J. 1997. "Instrument Relevance in Multivariate Linear Models: A Simple Measure." *Review of Economics and Statistics* 79 (2): 348–52.

Wacziarg, R., and J. S. Wallack. 2004. "Trade Liberalization and Intersectoral Labor Movements." *Journal of International Economics* 64: 411–39.

Wacziarg, R., and K. H. Welch. 2008. "Trade Liberalization and Growth: New Evidence." *World Bank Economic Review* 22 (2): 187–231.

CHAPTER 6

Conclusions and Policy Implications

Abstract

Labor mobility costs are particularly high in developing countries. For workers confronted by a trade shock, these costs will affect a worker's decision to remain in a job or change to a new job. In the aggregate, labor reallocation may be less than predicted if mobility costs are not taken into account. The result is sluggish or only partial adjustment because workers have sticky feet, and there is an associated adjustment cost arising from forgone gains to trade. The simulations in this study illustrate the adjustment paths employment and wages take in response to a negative sectoral trade shock; they predict long-run welfare gains even for workers in the affected sector, but only over a long adjustment period. Moreover, there is complementary evidence that trade liberalization ultimately increases employment and wages, helping to reduce poverty. But the presence of mobility costs will determine which workers are affected, and to what extent. That raises policy questions about how to facilitate and accelerate labor adjustment in order to maximize the gains from trade reform. This chapter explores policy options that act through various channels to reduce adjustment costs.

Main Findings

The estimates and simulations generated by the theoretical models used in this study confirm the findings of previous studies that trade liberalization improves aggregate welfare and is in the long run associated with higher employment and wages, and therefore poverty reduction.[1] The analysis presented here begins to address a major gap in the literature, which has heretofore provided limited evidence about the trade-related adjustment costs faced by workers in developing countries and how they are affected by mobility costs.

Conceptually, the presence of labor market frictions reduces the potential gains from trade reform. For a tariff reduction in a given sector, the resulting change in relative prices raises real wages in some sectors and reduces them in the liberalized sector. The emerging wage gaps lead to labor reallocation. But workers typically incur costs to change jobs—the higher the mobility costs, the slower the transition to the new labor market steady state. Workers' sticky feet result in forgone welfare gains from trade in terms of employment and earnings.

A primary contribution of the research reported here is the estimation of labor mobility costs across a large sample of developed and developing countries. This report presents an estimation strategy for capturing mobility costs when only net flows of workers between industries are observed; the strategy generates cross-country estimates that are internationally comparable.

The basic analytical approach is then refined to take advantage of micro-level data on worker transitions and wages when gross flows can be observed in order to derive mobility cost estimates that account for sector and formality status. These cost estimates are used to model dynamic labor adjustment between sectors and in and out of the labor force, the associated wage paths, and the resulting labor adjustment costs.

The main findings of this report are that

- *Labor mobility costs in developing countries are high.* The costs incurred by workers in developing economies are much higher than those of workers in developed economies.

- *Forgone trade gains due to frictions in labor mobility can also be substantial.* When labor adjustment with and without mobility costs is compared, the presence of mobility costs means that worker transitions are fewer and slower and fall short of the potential magnitude of total reallocation. As a result, some potential gains in terms of increased worker welfare are forgone. Higher mobility costs translate into higher adjustment costs.

- *Workers rather than firms bear the brunt of adjustment costs.* When a trade shock hits a developing country, the costs associated with worker decisions are notably higher than those associated with employer decisions. That is, the mobility costs borne by workers far outweigh the adjustment costs borne by firms. In Argentina, for example, simulation of a large, positive trade shock is shown to benefit firm profits proportionally more than worker wages.

- *Mobility costs and labor market adjustments to trade-related shocks vary by industry, firm type, and worker type.* Estimating mobility costs and subsequent labor market responses at a more disaggregated level to take account of, among other areas, sector, firm size and worker formality status, requires detailed panel data such as those from social security records and labor force surveys. The results illustrate the importance of accounting for heterogeneity.

- *Entry costs are significantly higher for formal than for informal employment,* based on evidence from Brazil, Mexico, and Morocco. Permanent trade shocks that reduce domestic prices can therefore be associated with increases in the share of informal employment due to higher labor force participation.

The informal sector seems to act as a stepping stone into formal employment, and total economy-wide employment can increase after episodes of trade liberalization (or any other permanent reduction in domestic prices).

- *Firm size can affect labor mobility costs.* For Morocco, finding employment in large firms was shown to be easier than in small firms. This result has implications for where workers find employment after a permanent trade shock; the relative increases in employment in larger firms outweigh those in smaller firms.

- Using regression analysis to validate the simulation model predictions, it was found that *structural reforms in developing countries increase economy-wide wages and employment* of workers who enter the formal labor force from informality. It appears that structural reforms have an impact on labor market outcomes as well as on growth.

- *Workers displaced by plant closings*, which can be caused by trade reforms or other trade-related shocks that reduce domestic prices in certain industries, *are likely to face long periods of reduced real wages*—longer than those of workers separated for other reasons. It takes about nine years for displaced workers in Mexico to recover their real wages after a plant closing.

Policy Implications

The findings here provide insights that could be helpful to policymakers hoping to mitigate negative short-term consequences of trade liberalization and facilitate labor adjustment in order to accelerate the transition to a competitive, trade-supportive labor market.

Although some distortive labor market policies, such as severance payments, might have been adopted with the objective of protecting workers, they may slow labor adjustment. However, because the removal of such distortions is politically sensitive, the potential effects should be carefully considered. Heckman and Pages (2000) suggested that removing excessive job protections could promote creation of new jobs. On the other hand, recent research on the influence of minimum wage and employment protection laws on wages, the distribution of wages, and employment suggests that these laws have less impact than previous studies had suggested.[2] Of course, unnecessary regulation that if adhered to might raise hiring and firing costs (thus reducing employment opportunities for workers) should be minimized, but in developing countries with high rates of informality, the costs to firms tend to be minimal.

The findings emerging from this analysis imply that it is time to pay more attention to the role of non-firm-related factors that generate labor mobility and adjustment costs. Because adjustment costs borne by employers as a result of such distortions tend to be quite small relative to the costs to workers themselves, policies should focus primarily on worker mobility costs. Governments should first consider policies that reduce mobility costs and then consider social assistance programs designed to accelerate worker employment transitions, thus lowering the adjustment costs of trade-related shocks.

The source of friction will determine the best policy to reduce the costs. For costs related to geographic relocation, for instance, compensation of moving expenses could be provided to workers showing proof of relocation, with the amount perhaps tied to the destination market. If workers are risk-averse about moving because they lack information about other job markets, job search assistance and labor exchanges could reduce information asymmetries and increase the probability of finding a job. If job search is costly, transitional income support—e.g., through unemployment benefits with a job search requirement—could facilitate the search process, particularly in single-earner households. If there is a skills mismatch, workers may wish to acquire new skills adapted to market demand. Because open-ended financing for skills upgrading that is not targeted may have little if any financial returns, training programs need to be carefully designed, targeted, and incentivized, for example, through cost sharing by the worker. When potential job losses are high or widespread, or are in regions afflicted by already high unemployment, temporary public works programs can provide partial replacement income to smooth household consumption and avoid severe welfare losses during a transitional period.

The simulation results of country-specific analysis using the Trade and Labor Adjustment Costs Toolkit can be used to test for potential effects of prospective trade policy changes. For example, the toolkit could be used to estimate the speed of adjustment and the magnitude of potential employment and wage gains and losses in all sectors of the economy (aggregated to a certain level) for a given tariff change or international price shock. However, although this information on the size of forgone gains to trade could help convince policymakers on the rationale for government intervention through adjustment assistance programs, it is not the right instrument for designing specific policy parameters. Additional considerations that will be important for effective policy design, such as understanding the country's existing and required administrative capacity and how policies would interface with current social protection programs, are beyond the scope of this report. The discussion that follows nevertheless describes a range of labor adjustment policies, lessons from specific country experiences and pros and cons associated with each, and generalized policy recommendations.[3]

The need for publicly funded labor adjustment programs rises with the total costs of adjustment. Since individual workers cannot anticipate trade shocks, the costs of adjustment cannot be fully internalized beforehand. But if workers could costlessly change jobs within and between industries, there would be no need for public intervention. Also, because developing country capital markets are imperfect, workers are unlikely to be able to find financing to cover inter-industry mobility costs. At the other extreme, if interventions are overly generous, adjustment may be thwarted. Labor adjustment programs should therefore be designed carefully or the benefits of current social protection programs enhanced to reduce mobility costs and thus facilitate adjustment. Moreover, labor adjustment programs used as compensation schemes could mobilize political support for trade reforms. Examples of potential policies as detailed in López-Acevedo and Savchenko (2013) are summarized below.

A Typology of Policies and Programs

Governments have a sophisticated toolbox of policies that can be used to address worker mobility costs, although most of them were not originally designed for this purpose. Table 6.1 summarizes policies that can alleviate the labor adjustment costs of trade liberalization and other trade-related shocks, broadly classified as labor market, trade, or other policies.

Labor market policies that can support workers affected by trade liberalization or related shocks consist of active labor market policies (ALMPs), passive labor market policies (PLMPs), and social protection policies. ALMPs help workers find new employment through job search assistance, subsidized employment, and upgrading or acquiring new skills. PLMPs include cash transfers to firms or workers affected by negative trade shocks as well as unemployment benefits or insurance. Social protection policies typically include health insurance, severance payments, and other means-tested income support programs.

Trade policies that could smooth labor adjustments and give workers time to transition after trade liberalization consist of gradual liberalization, early announcement of policy reforms, and temporary safeguards. For example, a major change in the trade policies of developed countries—cessation of the

Table 6.1 A Typology of Policies to Address Labor Adjustment Costs

Labor market policies	1. Active labor market policies (ALMPs)
	a. Training and acquisition of new skills
	b. Job search assistance
	c. Subsidized employment (short-term contracts for displaced workers; public works)
	2. Passive labor market policies (PLMPs)
	a. Direct subsidies to restructuring firms
	b. Direct compensation to workers
	c. Unemployment benefits or insurance
	3. Social protection policies
	a. Health insurance
	b. Severance payments
	c. General income support
Trade policies	1. Gradual liberalization
	2. Early announcement
	3. Safeguard measures
Other policies	1. Job creation in new sectors
	2. Education policies

Sources: López-Acevedo and Savchenko 2013; adapted from OECD 2005 and Jansen, Peters, and Salazar-Xirinachs 2011.

Multi Fibre Arrangement—was implemented gradually, starting in 1995 but not phased out completely until the end of 2004, and temporary safeguards for Chinese apparel exports were established to help other countries adjust to the phase-out. Similarly, most preferential trade agreements specify gradual phase-out for the most sensitive industries in participating countries.

Governments can use other policies to help workers adjust to trade shocks, such as stimulating employment in other industrial sectors or making educational systems more flexible and more connected to changing labor market needs. Many of these policies directly target labor mobility costs generated by skills mismatches, policy distortions, or geographical distribution.

A wide range of policies are used to address the skills mismatches of workers who are employed in industries adversely affected by trade liberalization and the demand for skills in new or growing industries. Many countries actively use (re) training programs and job search assistance to clear mismatches between demand and supply of skills. For example, the U.S. Trade Adjustment Assistance (US TAA) program offers workers affected by trade policies up to 130 weeks of remedial and vocational training. Many countries have job search assistance programs to help unemployed workers find jobs in new sectors, such as the US TAA and Austrian Steel Foundation programs. Unemployment insurance is also used to help workers cope with temporary shocks (e.g., the Brazilian Labor Market Reform of 1986). Early announcement of policy changes or gradual trade liberalization may create a time cushion for workers to adjust their skills and transition to other industries.

Direct compensation is sometimes used to address costs created by market distortions. For example, the European Union Common Agricultural Policy (EU CAP) switched from setting prices for agricultural produce, thereby distorting the market, to direct payments to compensate farmers affected by competition from foreign agricultural products.

Finally, many of the policies described in table 6.1 could help reduce the cost of geographic relocation of labor between regionally concentrated industries. Gradual liberalization, early announcement, and safeguard measures may give workers and firms the time to prepare for moving to other areas. Unemployment compensation could also help workers with relocating. Job creation in new sectors, public works, and short-term contracts in new locations may encourage workers to move. For example, the US TAA program reimburses workers for relocating to a job outside the local area.

Country Experiences

To provide guidance in policy design in terms of what has and has not worked, there is a need to document the experiences of labor adjustment assistance policies. In developed countries, trade adjustment assistance (TAA) policies typically have a long history and extensive tools. In developing countries, by contrast, simple social protection systems are often nonexistent, and introducing new programs is difficult both politically and financially.

What is needed is a clear understanding of the environments that shape the selection of programs.

Many developed countries have comprehensive programs to assist workers affected by trade liberalization. These programs encompass labor market interventions ranging from training and subsidies to counseling services. Usually these programs have been generously funded. Examples are the US TAA program, the EU CAP, and the Austrian Steel Foundation programs. They include direct compensation, such as the direct payments to EU farmers, and unemployment insurance and wage subsidies, as in the US TAA. These programs are complemented by ALMPs, such as retraining and job search assistance.

- The *US TAA* program is a federal program that helps workers to reduce trade-related adjustment costs generated by skills mismatch and distance to new jobs through a variety of policies, among them job search assistance, training, wage subsidies, health insurance for the unemployed, job search, and reallocation allowances. The program, founded in 1962, currently offers TAA for workers, farmers, firms, and communities. According to the U.S. Department of Labor, in 2011 about 200,000 workers used the US TAA. The program helps workers from any industry who have been displaced due to foreign trade, unlike the sector-specific EU and Austrian programs.

  Evaluations of the US TAA programs show mixed results, including limited effectiveness in helping trade-affected workers obtain reemployment at a suitable wage through training, temporary income support, and other services (Schochet et al. 2012).[4] The evaluations raise serious questions about what aspects of training may affect employment outcomes. US TAA recipients increased their use of reemployment services and of training and education, including acquiring educational credentials. Often, this was in lieu of seeking employment, and as expected the labor market outcomes for participants were significantly worse for the first two years after job loss than for a matched comparison group of nonrecipients. But in the final year of the follow-up period, though program participants had lower earnings than the comparison group, they worked about the same number of weeks (Schochet et al. 2012). This was particularly true for older participants. This is consistent with the findings of Decker and Corson (1995) and Reynolds and Palatucci (2008) that training has no effect on raising participant earnings. On the other hand, Berk (2012) concluded that impacts on employment and earnings were more favorable for program participants who received training than for those who received TAA income support without training, though trainees still earned significantly lower average hourly wages than their matched comparators. And among TAA participants who received occupational skills training, only 37 percent were employed in the occupations for which they trained (Schochet et al. 2012).

  Kletzer (2001) argues that a stronger social safety net than the US TAA provides would diminish worker opposition to further trade liberalization by alleviating anxieties about job displacement. Critics have also asserted that the TAA fails to address the most critical component of workers' costs: earnings losses after reemployment. Given the weak evidence about retraining programs and findings that the best retraining is delivered on the job, other programs, such as wage insurance as proposed by Kletzer (2001), would "encourage workers to be reemployed rapidly while improving their access to on-the-job training."

- The *EU CAP* introduced compensation in the late 1960s to protect farmers from foreign competition. The program has undergone several transformations, such as introduction of direct payments to farmers and reduction of agricultural support prices (the support was originally administered through import tariffs, export refunds, and quotas). These reforms represented a shift from price controls to direct compensation. Analyses of CAP effectiveness found that while farm incomes increased, in the long run CAP did not protect agricultural employment. Moreover, rather than providing compensation to farmers with low incomes, the farmers who had benefited most from the previous price setting were often the most productive farms (Swinnen and Van Herck 2010).

- The main objective of the *Austrian Steel Foundation* is to help displaced workers find new work since the Austrian steel industry was privatized; it offers a wide range of services, including vocational orientation programs, small business start-up assistance, extensive training and retraining, formal education, and job search assistance. Even though the program was not designed to deal with adjustments associated with a trade shock, the permanent privatization of the industry was very similar to a reform of trade policy. The foundation is financed by all participating parties: the trainees themselves, the firms, local government through unemployment benefits, and the remaining workers in the steel industry who pay a solidarity share of their gross wages to the foundation. An impact evaluation found the program to be successful in achieving its goals, with the trainees having a higher probability of being employed than the control group five years after leaving the program (Winter-Ebmer 2001).

In developing countries, TAA programs tend to be piecemeal and less systematic. The few documented programs point to specific interventions (either training or retraining, wage subsidies, or job search assistance) that were put in place to compensate workers or firms for a structural shock but were later integrated into the safety net programs of a given country. However, these programs seem not to be part of a comprehensive set of policies; instead they are mainly implemented ad hoc. Programs have been created to help workers transition after trade liberalization (Brazilian Labor Market Reform of 1986, Mexico's PROCAMPO); address the consequences of temporary shocks (Argentina's REPRO); or facilitate employment of vulnerable groups (Mexico's Probecat). Impact evaluations of training programs in Latin America and the Caribbean (Ibarraran and Rosas

Shady 2009) suggest that these programs have had little impact on the probability of finding employment.

- *Mexico's PROCAMPO* program was established in 1993–94 to compensate crop producers expected to see prices decline after initiation of the North American Free Trade Agreement. It is now the largest agricultural program in Mexico, providing farmers with per-hectare cash transfers that are decoupled from land use. Cord and Wodon (2001) found that PROCAMPO had a positive effect on poverty reduction and a multiplier effect on household income: one peso of PROCAMPO cash transfer resulted in a two-peso increase in household impact.

- *Brazil's Labor Market Reform of 1986*, which predated trade liberalization in 1991, established unemployment insurance, employment subsidies, and ALMPs. The reform was designed to establish new social support programs or build up those already in existence. The programs were later used by individuals affected by trade liberalization. The universal unemployment insurance coverage targeted people who involuntarily lost formal jobs, and the employment subsidy program consisted of government transfers to workers with wages under a certain threshold. The reform also introduced training and job search assistance. Evaluations of labor market outcomes of those who did and did not collect unemployment insurance found no significant difference in wages (Cunningham 2000).

- Established in 2002 in response to the economic crisis, the main goal of *REPRO in Argentina* is to protect workers from massive layoffs that might be triggered by economic shocks. The program targets workers in specific industries and geographic areas by providing temporary support to enterprises. Affected firms apply for financing for no more than one year and then disburse the funds to workers. Trucco and Tussie (2012) conclude that the program was successful in preventing massive layoffs.

- In response to the 1982 economic crisis, in 1984 the Mexican government established *Probecat* for the unemployed who live mostly in urban areas. The main services it provided were training and subsistence allowances during the training period. Training had three modules: school-based, in-service, and for the self-employed. Despite positive initial results (Revenga, Riboud, and Tan 1994), after accounting for self-selection into the program, Ravallion and Wodon (1998) did not find a statistically significant effect on either employment or wages.

General Lessons for Policy Design

Well-targeted labor adjustment assistance programs that have appropriate incentives could be effective at facilitating labor adjustment by reducing mobility costs. Labor market policies already in place are often used as instruments for adjustment assistance, but the nature of the adjustment costs generated by trade-related shocks is quite different from the costs generated by other economic shocks. For one thing, trade liberalization shocks are permanent and industry-specific—recall the longer adjustment period for Mexican workers displaced by plant closures. That is why adjustment programs oriented to changing the skill composition of workers affected by trade liberalization, such as training them in skills demanded by emerging industries, may be more appropriate.

Governments should look to policies that reduce labor mobility costs and put in place social assistance programs designed to accelerate worker employment transitions, thus lowering the adjustment costs of trade-related shocks. The best policy design would focus on minimizing mobility costs and accelerating employment transitions. This could mean, for example, offering workers retraining programs or financial relocation assistance. Programs that would alleviate adjustment costs but not prevent the economy-wide restructuring that accompanies trade liberalization are second-best to programs that facilitate mobility if, in effect, the former act as disincentives to moving.

The following general lessons to inform policy design can be drawn from the experiences of both developed and developing countries:

- **Context-specific:** Concentrating on specific sectors (Mexico PROCAMPO) or using only specific instruments (Argentina REPRO) may be more effective than spreading resources thinly across multiple labor adjustment assistance programs. Therefore, the design of effective adjustment assistance in developing countries should be context specific. Comprehensive programs with a variety of support instruments (similar to the US TAA program) may be attractive but could be costly for developing countries.

- **Minimizing distortions:** How to minimize the distortions that might be created by labor adjustment programs should be analyzed carefully. For example, setting agricultural produce prices to protect farmers from competition from foreign produce created market distortions in the EU. That policy was later amended to eliminate the distortions.

- **Cost sharing:** Different cost-sharing options for trade adjustment policies should be considered. For instance, the Austrian Steel Foundation is financed by all parties: trainees, firms, local governments, and unaffected workers in the industry.

- **Design of retraining:** Given their generally poor track record, any retraining programs must be designed carefully. Retraining programs tend to be expensive yet provide only small improvements in terms of employment and virtually no improvements in the earnings of program participants compared to displaced nonparticipants. A notable exception is the training program of the Austrian Steel Foundation, which has a unique cost-sharing financial model.

- **Wage insurance or subsidies:** Theoretical models predict that wage subsidies for workers who move to expanding from shrinking sectors could be an efficient way to compensate losers at the lowest cost. Impact evaluations of labor market policies have found examples in which wage subsidies increased the probability of employment for those subsidized. Moreover, on-the-job training tends to be more effective than other training programs, and wage insurance or subsidies would accelerate access to this type of training.

Notes

1. See, for example, Winters, McCulloch, and McKay (2004).
2. See Betcherman (2012) and World Bank (2012).
3. More specific policy recommendations would require extensive evaluations of labor adjustment policies around the world and their suitability to particular countries and sectors.
4. The Employment and Training Administration of the United States Department of Labor funded a comprehensive evaluation of the TAA program to document its implementation and assess its ability to achieve its goal of helping participants find rapid and suitable reemployment. The evaluation included a nationally representative impact analysis in which TAA program recipients were matched to a comparison group, and education, employment, earnings, and other outcomes were examined for the four years after job loss.

References

Berk, J. 2012. *Understanding the Employment Outcomes of Trainees in the Trade Adjustment Assistance (TAA) Program under the 2002 Amendments*. Princeton, NJ: Mathematica Policy Research.

Betcherman, G. 2012. "Labor Market Institutions: A Review of the Literature." Policy Research Working Paper 6276, World Bank, Washington, DC.

Cord, L., and Q. Wodon. 2001. "Do Mexico's Agricultural Programs Alleviate Poverty? Evidence from the Ejido Sector." *Cuadernos de Economía* 38 (114): 239–56.

Cunningham, W. V. 2000. "Unemployment Insurance in Brazil: Unemployment Duration, Wages, and Sectoral Choice." Unpublished manuscript, World Bank, Latin America and Caribbean Region Social Protection Sector, Washington, DC.

Decker, P. T., and W. Corson. 1995. "International Trade and Worker Displacement: Evaluation of the Trade Adjustment Assistance Program." *Industrial and Labor Relations Review* 48 (4): 758–74.

Heckman, J. J., and C. Pages. 2000. "The Cost of Job Security Regulation: Evidence from Latin American Labor Markets." NBER Working Paper 7773, National Bureau of Economic Research, Cambridge, MA.

Ibarraran, P., and D. Rosas Shady. 2009. "Evaluating the Impact of Job Training Programmes in Latin America: Evidence from IDB-Funded Operations." *Journal of Development Effectiveness* 1 (2): 195–206.

Jansen, M., R. Peters, and J. M. Salazar-Xirinachs. 2011. *Trade and Employment: From Myths to Facts*. Geneva: International Labour Organization.

Kletzer, L. G. 2001. "A Prescription to Relieve Worker Anxiety." Policy Brief 01-2, Peterson Institute for International Economics, Washington, DC.

López-Acevedo, G., and Y. Savchenko. 2013. "Trade Adjustment Assistance Programs." Unpublished manuscript, International Trade Department, Poverty Reduction and Economic Management, World Bank, Washington, DC.

OECD. 2005. *OECD Employment Outlook.* Paris: Organisation for Economic Co-operation and Development.

Ravallion, M., and Q. Wodon. 1998. "Evaluating a Targeted Social Program when Placement Is Decentralized." Policy Research Working Paper 1945, World Bank, Washington, DC.

Revenga, A., M. Riboud, and H. Tan. 1994. "The Impact of Mexico's Retraining Program on Employment and Wages." *World Bank Economic Review* 8 (2): 247–77.

Reynolds, K. M., and J. S. Palatucci. 2008. "Does Trade Adjustment Assistance Make a Difference?" Working Paper 2008-12, American University, Washington, DC.

Schochet, P. Z., R. D'Amico, J. Berk, S. Dolfin, and N. Wozny. 2012. *Estimated Impacts for Participants in the Trade Adjustment Assistance (TAA) Program under the 2002 Amendments.* Princeton, NJ: Mathematica Policy Research.

Swinnen, J. F. M., and K. Van Herck. 2010. "Compensation Payments in EU Agriculture." In *Trade Adjustment Costs in Developing Countries: Impacts, Determinants and Policy Responses,* edited by G. Porto and B. M. Hoekman, 361–81. Washington, DC: International Bank for Reconstruction and Development/World Bank.

Trucco, P., and D. Tussie. 2012. "Learning from Past Battles in Argentina? The Role of REPRO in the Prevention of Crisis-induced Lay-Offs." GTA Analytical Paper 7, Center for Economic Policy Research, Global Trade Alert, Washington, DC.

Wacziarg, R., and K. H. Welch. 2008. "Trade Liberalization and Growth: New Evidence." *World Bank Economic Review* 22 (2): 187–231.

Winter-Ebmer, R. 2001. "Evaluation of an Innovative Redundancy-Retraining Project: The Austrian Steel Foundation." CEPR Discussion Paper Series 2776, Centre for Economic Policy Research, London.

Winters, A., N. McCulloch, and A. McKay. 2004. "Trade Liberalization and Poverty: The Evidence So Far." *Journal of Economic Literature* 42 (1): 72–115.

World Bank. 2012. *Jobs: World Development Report 2013.* Washington, DC: International Bank for Reconstruction and Development/World Bank.

The Analytical Framework

A Model of Labor Mobility Costs

The model of labor mobility costs is based on the equilibrium labor mobility framework of Artuç, Chaudhuri, and McLaren (2010) and the background paper by Artuç, Lederman, and Porto (2013). In the model, workers can move across sectors at a cost. There are N sectors in the economy, including traded as well as nontraded sectors.[1] The economy is composed of L agents. At a given point, each agent is employed in a sector and earns the market wage in that sector. Instantaneous utility, u, of a worker employed in sector i at time t is defined as:

$$u_t^i = w_t^i + \eta^i, \tag{1}$$

where w_t^i is the observed sector-specific wage and η^i is a sector-specific fixed nonpecuniary benefit, such as happiness. Both components of the instantaneous utility are identical for all workers in a given sector.[2] η^i can best be interpreted as compensating differentials across sectors. As argued below, these compensating differentials are important to the identification of mobility costs. The agent observes both w_t^i and η^i, but only w_t^i is observed in the data.

At the end of each time period t, the agent chooses a sector of employment for the next time period, $t + 1$. However, switching industries is costly and workers cannot freely choose the sector with the highest instantaneous utility. Thus workers pay a mobility cost if they decide to move. The mobility cost has two components, one that is identical for all workers moving from industry i to industry j ($C^{i,j}$), and another random idiosyncratic component that is different for every worker in an industry in every time period ($\varepsilon_t^{i,j}$). Thus, when a worker moves from sector i to j, she pays the fixed moving cost $C^{i,j}$ and the random idiosyncratic cost $\varepsilon_t^{i,j} = \varepsilon_t^i - \varepsilon_t^j$. The random variable ε has an extreme value distribution with the scale parameter υ (the scale parameter is proportional to the standard error).

Workers choose the optimal sector dynamically. Agents are risk-neutral, have rational expectations, live infinitely, and have the same discount factor, $\beta < 1$. Let V_t^i be the expected present discounted utility of an agent currently employed in sector i, taking wages, fixed utility, and future values into account. The worker's optimization problem can be characterized by the Bellman equation:

$$V_t^i = w_t^i + \eta^i + \beta E_t \max_j \left\{ V_{t+1}^j - C^{i,j} - \varepsilon_t^{i,j} \right\}. \tag{2}$$

The Bellman equation can be rearranged as

$$V_t^i = w_t^i + \eta^i + \beta E_t V_{t+1}^i + \beta \Omega_{t+1}^i, \tag{3}$$

where Ω_{t+1}^i is the option value of moving, equal to the expected benefit of moving conditional on the net benefit of moving being positive. The option value of moving can be solved analytically when the random variable ε_t^i is distributed iid extreme value (see Artuç, Chaudhuri, and McLaren [2010] for further details).

Thanks to McFadden (1973), labor flows can be expressed as

$$m_t^{i,j} = \frac{\exp\left(\left(E_t V_{t+1}^j - E_t V_{t+1}^i - C^{i,j} \right) \frac{1}{\nu} \right)}{\sum_{k=1}^N \exp\left(\left(E_t V_{t+1}^k - E_t V_{t+1}^i - C^{i,k} \right) \frac{1}{\nu} \right)}, \tag{4}$$

where $m_t^{i,j}$ is the gross share of workers moving to sector j from sector i at time period t.

Finally, the allocation of labor of each sector is given by

$$L_{t+1}^j = \sum_{k \neq j} m_t^{k,j} L_t^k + m_t^{j,j} L_t^j, \tag{5}$$

where L_t^i is the total number of workers in sector i. In consequence, the model generates multilateral flows of workers across all sectors of the economy. This structure makes it possible to estimate the key moving cost parameters by matching the predictions of the model with the data.

Estimating Labor Mobility Costs

Different estimation techniques can be used with the model depending on the data available. The parameters of interest are the mobility cost, $C^{i,j}$, and the variance proportionality factor, ν.

First, Artuç, Chaudhuri, and McLaren (2010) showed how this model (assuming an exogenous discount factor β) reduces to

$$\left(\ln m_t^{i,j} - \ln m_t^{i,i} \right) - \beta \left(\ln m_{t+1}^{i,j} - \ln m_{t+1}^{i,i} \right) = \frac{-(1-\beta)}{\nu} C^{i,j} + \frac{\beta}{\nu} \left(w_{t+1}^j - w_{t+1}^i \right) + \mu_{t+1}. \tag{6}$$

In practice, the equation is estimated as

$$\left(\ln m_t^{i,j} - \ln m_t^{i,i} \right) - \beta \left(\ln m_{t+1}^{i,j} - \ln m_{t+1}^{i,i} \right) = \alpha + \gamma \left(w_{t+1}^j - w_{t+1}^i \right) + \mu_{t+1}. \tag{7}$$

The resulting expressions for C and v as functions of the estimated coefficients are therefore $v = \dfrac{\beta}{\gamma}$ and $C = \dfrac{\alpha v}{-(1-\beta)}$. The authors suggest estimating this equation with the Generalized Method of Moments (GMM) estimator using the past values of flows and wages as instruments. In practice, the results are compared to the Ordinary Least Squares (OLS) estimates. Although the model lacks enough degrees of freedom to estimate the full set of $C^{i,j}$ parameters, average entry costs for all initial sectors i into sector j can be identified, i.e., sector-specific entry costs, C^{j}. This model is designed to be used with panel data of workers to construct the transition matrices, in which the gross flows of jobs, $m_{t}^{i,j}$, between sectors can be observed. In practice, however, only the transition matrices are needed to implement this approach, not the underlying data.

Second, Artuç, Lederman, and Porto (2013) showed how to estimate labor mobility costs when true panel data for individuals are not available and thus gross flows of workers are unobservable. Instead, they use time series of net industry flows. They propose a simulation estimator where the labor allocations simulated with the structural model are compared with the labor allocations observed in the data. Concretely, the authors define a minimum distance estimator that matches changes in employment allocations for all sectors across time:

$$\hat{C/v} = \arg\min_{C/v} \sum_{t=1}^{T-1}\sum_{i=2}^{N} w_{t}^{i}\left(\left(\tilde{L}_{t+1}^{i}\left(C/v;\eta,u^{*}\right) - \tilde{L}_{t}^{i}\left(C/v;\eta,u^{*}\right)\right) - \left(L_{t+1}^{i} - L_{t}^{i}\right)\right)^{2},$$

(8)

where $\tilde{L}^{i}$ are the employment predictions of the model and w_{t}^{i} are weights used for efficiency. Implementing the estimator starts with guesses for the ratio of mobility costs to the variance of the utility shocks, C/v, the compensating differentials for the manufacturing sectors, η^{i}, and the utility differentials for the residual sector, u_{t}^{*}. Given these guesses, the model is solved with backwards iteration. Then it is possible to calculate the gross flows of workers, $m_{t}^{i,j}$, and predict the next period's labor allocation:

$$\tilde{L}_{t+1}^{j} = \sum_{i=i}^{K} \tilde{L}_{t}^{i} m_{t}^{i,j},$$

(9)

where $\tilde{L}_{t+1}^{j} = L_{t}^{j}$ for $t = 1$. The predictions are then compared with the data and the guesses are updated until convergence. To achieve efficiency, the model is estimated in two steps: first, the identity matrix is used as the weighting matrix ω_{t}^{i}, then for the second step the residuals from this first step are plugged into ω_{t}^{i}. This approach identifies only an average or uniform moving cost for all sectors across all years as a ratio of the variance of the utility shocks, C/v. Assuming the $v = 1$, given the convention of normalizing wages, the estimates should be interpreted as mobility costs in terms of the average real wage in each country.

Third, Kaplan, Lederman, and Robertson (2013) followed a two-step estimation procedure suggested by Artuç (2013) for panel data of workers when gross flows of jobs across industries can be observed. The first stage involves a Poisson regression in which the dependent variable is the number of workers moving from sector i to sector j. Independent variables include three dummy variables: a dummy for the sending sector, α_t^i, a dummy for the receiving sector, λ_t^j, and a dummy equal to one for all different sector pairs, $1_{i \neq j}$. The first stage equation is

$$L_t^i m_t^{i,j} = \exp\left(\alpha_t^i + \lambda_t^j + \delta_t^j 1_{i \neq j}\right) + e_t^{i,j}, \tag{10}$$

where the coefficient is $\delta_t^j = \dfrac{-C_t^j}{v}$. Estimated coefficients from the first stage are then combined to generate the variables for the second-stage estimation of the Bellman equation. The variable for the option value of moving is calculated as $\tilde{\Omega}_t^i = -\lambda_t^i - \alpha_t^i + \log(L_t^i)$ and the dependent variable can then be constructed as $\psi_t^{i,j} = \left(\lambda_t^i - \lambda_t^j\right) - \beta\left(\lambda_{t+1}^i - \lambda_{t+1}^j\right) - \beta\left(\tilde{\Omega}_t^i - \tilde{\Omega}_t^j\right)$. Thus the estimated Bellman equation is

$$\psi_t^{i,j} = \phi\left(w_{t+1}^i - w_{t+1}^j\right) + \tilde{\eta}^i - \tilde{\eta}^j + z_t^{i,j}, \tag{11}$$

which is estimated directly with GMM using the past values of flows and wages as instruments. The estimates from the second stage allow the recovery of v, which is then combined with the estimates from the first stage to get an estimate of the actual adjustment costs. Like Artuç, Chaudhuri, and McLaren (2010), sector-specific entry costs can be identified. However, one benefit of this estimation strategy is that the sector-specific entry costs can be estimated for every year, that is, C_t^j. It also allows for a finer disaggregation of sectors because the estimation strategy is better equipped to handle zero values, which are more likely to arise as the number of industry transition pairs increases. It also allows for more accurate estimation of the underlying structural parameters.

Simulating the Effects of Trade-Related Shocks

The final step of the analysis framework is to use the estimates of labor mobility costs, C, to simulate labor market responses to a trade-related shock and derive measures of adjustment costs. However, to simulate the economy, it is necessary to add more structure to the model.

On the demand side, preferences are assumed to be Cobb-Douglas:

$$u_t = \Pi_i (x_t^i)^{\theta^i}, \tag{12}$$

where x_t^i is the consumption of output from sector i at time t and θ^i is the sector's share of total expenditure. This can be inferred from data on household budget shares (from household surveys) or the share of each sector in total consumption (generally available from input-output tables).

Next, production functions are used to infer labor demand. Production functions are also assumed to be Cobb-Douglas:

$$Q_t^i = A^i (K_t^i)^{\alpha_i} (L_t^i)^{1-\alpha_i}, \tag{13}$$

where Q_t^i is physical output of industry i, A^i is a technology parameter, K_t^i is capital, and L_t^i is labor. Labor is imperfectly mobile because workers can only move across sectors after paying the moving cost, C. Capital is assumed to be fixed, as in Artuç, Chaudhuri, and McLaren (2010).[3] The parameters, α_i, are approximated with the share of the wage bill in value added at the sector level. Assuming each sector pays a wage equal to the marginal product of labor, from the production function, the real wage equations can be derived as

$$w_t^i = \frac{p_t^i}{p_t} \tilde{A}^i (L_t^i)^{\alpha_i - 1}, \tag{14}$$

where P_t is the aggregate price index, p_t^i is the unit price of sector i's output, and $\tilde{A}^i = A^i (K^i)^{1-\alpha_i}$.

The model is closed with the following consumer price index equation:

$$P_t = \Pi_i (p_t^i)^{\theta^i} \tag{15}$$

with consumption shares θ^i.

Arias-Vázquez et al. (2013) also assumed that formal and informal sector products are identical and informal and formal workers are substitutes. However, informal workers are less productive than formal workers, consistent with their lower informal wages. That is, effective total human capital in industry i is

$$L_t^i = \sum_s a^s L_{t,}^s \tag{16}$$

where a^s is the productivity parameter of type s workers (formal or informal).

The production and demand functions are first used to calibrate the initial steady state of the economy. Then, a particular sector, i, is assumed to face an exogenous and unexpected percentage decline in its output price due to policy changes or external shocks. When the shock hits the economy, the transition path of employment allocations and wages to the new steady state is solved. Labor mobility costs enter into the model since labor allocations are a function of C.

Measuring Labor Adjustment Costs

Labor adjustment costs are measured using the preceding analytical framework to calculate the difference in workers' welfare between the potential post-shock equilibrium outcome with zero mobility costs and the actual post-shock equilibrium with non-zero mobility costs.

Recall that a worker's welfare has three separate components: her real wage, a sector-specific fixed nonpecuniary benefit, and an option value (which captures the possibility of moving to a different sector with a higher wage). The measure of welfare used is V_t^i, the expected present discounted utility of an agent currently employed in sector i at time t given by equation (3). Labor adjustment costs for workers in the food and beverages sector refer to a random worker who may or may not switch sectors.

The value V_{pre} corresponds to the welfare of the food and beverages worker before the shock. In the absence of mobility costs, after the shock the worker's welfare would immediately increase to the new steady-state value, V_{max}. In this scenario, there would be gains to trade upon impact, and these potential gains (PG) would be denoted

$$PG = V_{max} - V_{pre}. \tag{17}$$

When there are mobility costs, the worker cannot reach the higher welfare value, V_{max}, immediately because adjustment is sluggish. In fact, the actual welfare value, V, that a food and beverages worker can achieve along the adjustment path may be higher or lower than the initial welfare value, V_{pre}, because it depends on the wage path and the option value. On the one hand, wages in the shock-affected sector will fall at t_0 and gradually rise as workers move out of the sector. On the other hand, the option value will rise immediately, given that there is an increase in real wages in all other sectors. Therefore, the worker will be better off if the increase in the option value and the subsequent increases in wages dominate the initial decrease in wages that occurs in t_0. (Figure 3.5 assumes that the positive effects dominate even at t_0, showing an immediate increase in the welfare of the worker following the shock.) The increase in welfare over time reflects the actual gains to trade (G) for the worker, given as

$$G = V - V_{pre}. \tag{18}$$

Mobility costs prevent the worker from achieving welfare level V_{max}. Instead the worker only achieves V, and the resulting difference in welfare relative to the scenario without mobility costs is the labor adjustment cost, LAC, represented by the difference between the potential and actual gains from trade:

$$LAC = PG - G = V_{max} - V. \tag{19}$$

Adjustment costs can therefore be described as the difference between the optimal (in the absence of adjustment frictions) and the actual factor utilization levels.

Reduced-Form Analysis of the Impact of Structural Reform on Labor Outcomes

Testing econometrically for the impact of reforms on labor market outcomes begins by estimating the cross-country averages of each labor market outcome variable relative to the reform year using a regression of the labor market outcome variable of interest on dummy variables for each year on either side of the reform. The specification is

$$Y_{i,t} = \beta_0 + \beta_1 X_{i,t} + \sum_{j=-10}^{-1} \gamma_j PreDummy(j)_{i,t} + \sum_{j=1}^{10} \gamma_j PostDummy(j)_{i,t} + v_i + \varepsilon_{i,t}, \quad (20)$$

where Y is the labor-market outcome variable, i denotes the country, t denotes the year, X includes control variables if specified, $PreDummy(j)$ is a dummy variable equal to 1 j years before the reform, $PostDummy(j)$ is a dummy variable equal to 1 j years after the reform, v is the fixed effect, and ε is the idiosyncratic error. Time is equal to –1 the year before reform, 0 the year of reform, 1 the year after reform, etc. Each coefficient represents the average level of the dependent variable in its corresponding time period relative to the average level in the year of reform. The controls in all regressions include real GDP and working-age population as well as the labor force participation rate, except for the regression in which it appears as the dependent variable.

Endogeneity is tackled by using a two-stage fixed effects instrumental variables regression. The specification for the second stage is

$$Y_{i,t} = \beta_0 + \beta_1 X_{i,t} + \beta_2 time_{i,t} + \beta_3 \left(time_{i,t} \right)^2 + \beta_4 POST_{i,t} + v_i + \varepsilon_{i,t}, \quad (21)$$

where $time$ is the time trend and $POST$ is a dummy variable that takes the value 1 every year after the reform and 0 otherwise. Since it can be endogenous to the labor-market outcome variables, $POST$ is instrumented for in the first stage. The specification is

$$POST_{i,t} = \beta_0 + \beta_1 X_{i,t} + \beta_2 time_{i,t} + \beta_3 \left(time_{i,t} \right)^2 + \beta_4 IV_{i,t} + v_i + \varepsilon_{i,t}, \quad (22)$$

where IV is any combination of the instrumental variables, which are external debt-to-GDP ratio, terms of trade, 5-year change in a country's democracy score, and a 1-year lagged endogenous dummy variable. The predicted values for $POST$ from the first stage are then used in the second stage.

Reduced-Form Analysis of the Impact of Displacement on Labor Outcomes

The following specification is estimated to compare the average labor market outcomes of different types of separated workers with the benchmark category of non-separated workers:

$$Y_{i,t} = \delta_t + X'_{i,t}\beta + \sum_d \alpha_d TD_{i,d} + \varepsilon_{i,t}, \quad (23)$$

where Y represents the labor market outcome (log of real wages, hours of work, formality status, and tenure), δ_t is a time fixed effect, and X includes a rich set of covariates, including gender, marital status, state and industry fixed effects, education, age, and age squared. The variable of interest is TD, which reflects the type of separation, including plant closings, quitting, involuntary separation, and employers and self-employed who close their businesses. The omitted category is non-separated workers.

To investigate the existence of temporary and permanent effects of job displacement on current labor market outcomes, the specification is modified by adding lagged indicators of the type of displacement:

$$Y_{i,t} = \delta_t + X'_{i,t}\beta + \sum_{d,s=0}^{d,s=10} \alpha_{d,s} TD_{i,d,t-s} + \varepsilon_{i,t} \tag{24}$$

up to $s = 10$ years after displacement.

The model for the duration of unemployment that follows job displacement is a parametric hazard model. Assuming a Weibull distribution for the hazard function, the following model is estimated:

$$h(u) = \alpha\lambda^\alpha u^{\alpha-1} \tag{25}$$

with the survival function, $S(u) = exp(-(\lambda u)^\alpha)$, representing the probability that the period of unemployment is a length that is at least $U = u$. In other words, $S(u) = 1 - F(u) = \text{Prob}(U \geq u)$ with $F(\cdot)$ being the Weibull cumulative distribution function. The Weibull density function is given as $f(u) = \alpha\lambda u^{\alpha-1}e^{-\lambda u}$. The covariates in the hazard function are included by defining:

$$\lambda_{i,t} = e^{\delta_t + X'_{i,t}\beta + \sum_{d,s=0}^{d,s=10} \alpha_{d,s} TD_{i,d,t-s} + \varepsilon_{i,t}}. \tag{26}$$

The shape parameter of the Weibull distribution, α, defines the time dependence of the model and is the parameter of interest. The hazard rate is monotonically decreasing with $\alpha < 0$ and increasing with $\alpha > 0$.

Notes

1. In other settings, a residual sector could also be included for unemployment or informality.

2. This is an unavoidable assumption when at the industry level only aggregate data are available, as in chapter 3. However, this assumption can be relaxed when individual worker panel data are available, as in chapter 4. Heterogeneity could exist, for example, across workers in different sized firms or of different formality status.

3. This assumption is relaxed in Artuç, Lederman, and Porto (2013).

References

Arias-Vázquez, F. J., E. Artuç, D. Lederman, and D. Rojas. 2013. "Trade, Informal Employment and Labor Adjustment Costs." Policy Research Working Paper 6614, World Bank, Washington, DC.

Artuç, E. 2013. "Estimating Dynamic Discrete Choice Models with Unspecified Aggregate Shocks." Policy Research Working Paper 6480, World Bank, Washington, DC.

Artuç, E., S. Chaudhuri, and J. McLaren. 2010. "Trade Shocks and Labor Adjustment: A Structural Empirical Approach." *American Economic Review* 100: 1008–45.

Artuç, E., D. Lederman, and G. Porto. 2013. "A Mapping of Labor Mobility Costs in the Developing World." Policy Research Working Paper 6556, World Bank, Washington, DC.

Kaplan, D. S., D. Lederman, and R. Robertson. 2013. "Worker-Level Adjustment Costs in a Developing Country: Evidence from Mexico." Unpublished manuscript, International Trade Department, Poverty Reduction and Economic Management, World Bank, Washington, DC.

McFadden, D. 1973. "Conditional Logit Analysis of Qualitative Choice Behavior." In *Frontiers in Econometrics*, edited by P. Zarembka. New York: Academic Press.

Data Description and Sources

Average Labor Mobility and Adjustment Costs

Artuç, Chaudhuri, and McLaren (2008) derived estimates of labor mobility costs using panel data to build measures of gross employment flows across sectors. In many countries, however, the necessary panel data are not available. Instead, to estimate the model in chapter 3, data on aggregate net flows of workers across sectors and of intersectoral wage changes are used. These changes can be easily estimated from time series of sector-level employment and wages. A good source of this type of data is the United Nations Industrial Development Organization (UNIDO) Industrial Statistics Database for the period 1990–2008, which is available for many countries. The dataset provides information on number of establishments, number of employees, wages, output, value added, and gross fixed capital formation for industries with International Standard Industry Classification codes between 100 and 399. Artuç, Lederman, and Porto (2013) used UNIDO information on employment and wages for the estimation and also value added for the simulations. For the estimation, the data are aggregated into eight major manufacturing sectors: metals and minerals, chemicals and petroleum products, machinery, food and beverages, wood products, textiles and clothing, miscellaneous equipment, and motor vehicles. From these data, time series for the wage streams and the labor allocations were built for each sector and year. The UNIDO data have a good coverage of the manufacturing sector but not the nonmanufacturing sector. To overcome this limitation, national accounts data were used to construct measures of labor allocations in the nonmanufacturing sector. However, wages are not observed for the nonmanufacturing sector, and are therefore calibrated from the data. The methodology requires consecutive observations for several years without any missing data for the observed sectors. The resulting sample covers 25 developing and 22 developed countries, which are used for comparisons and descriptive regression analysis to estimate the correlates of average country labor mobility costs.

The estimation strategy of chapter 3 can only recover the average labor mobility cost across all industries in the economy. These estimates are sufficient if the policy analyst is interested in aggregate labor market responses to trade-related shocks. However, social security records and labor force surveys can be used to estimate labor mobility costs (and subsequent labor market responses) at a more disaggregated level. This cannot be done with the UNIDO data, because detailed data are needed on job flows and wages, not only at the industry level, but also for different types of firms or workers. And even in cases where richer data are available, the heterogeneity in the data is often limited. Chapter 4 therefore provides separate case studies that employ the richer datasets that are available for some countries.

Comparing Capital Adjustment and Labor Mobility Costs

To estimate the capital adjustment costs of firms and the labor mobility costs of workers in chapter 4, Artuç, Lederman, and Porto (2013) used firm- and household-level survey panel data for Argentina. Estimation of the firms' problem requires panel data with detailed information on the investment decisions of a firm—data on purchases of new capital as well as on sales of installed capital. The Argentine manufacturing survey, the *Encuesta Industrial Anual* (Annual Industrial Survey, EIA), meets these requirements. The EIA is a balanced panel of 568 Argentine manufacturing plants for the period 1994–2001. The EIA dataset provides information on gross revenues, costs, intermediate inputs, employment, consumption of energy and fuels, inventory stock, and both gross expenditures and gross sales of capital. Information on gross capital sales is important in order to estimate the role of partial irreversibility in the capital adjustment costs structure. Estimation of the workers' problem requires panel data on sectoral wages and gross flows of workers across sectors. The *Encuesta Permanente de Hogares* (Permanent Household Survey, EPH) meets these requirements; the database contains information on individual wages, employment sector, demographic characteristics, and other standard variables in labor force surveys. Part of the EPH is a panel used to track labor employment flows across sector pairs and average sector wages across six sectors for 1996–2007.

Case Studies of Sector Adjustment Costs

To estimate mobility costs across different industries in Mexico (chapter 4), Kaplan, Lederman, and Robertson (2013) used raw data from the Mexican Social Security Institute (*Instituto Mexicano del Seguro Social*, IMSS). IMSS is the agency that manages the social security accounts for all private sector tax-registered workers in Mexico. Since filing with the IMSS has been used as a criterion for formal sector participation, the data can be thought of as a census of private formal-sector establishments. The IMSS uses its own four digit industry classification system consisting of 271 separate industries that span all economic activity in the formal sector. Unfortunately, if employees leave the formal (tax-registered) sector, it is not possible to observe whether they become unemployed or find an informal job.

To estimate mobility costs for workers of different informality status in Brazil, Mexico, and Morocco (chapter 4), Arias-Vázquez et al. (2013) used labor force surveys from each country. The common feature among the surveys is the rotating panel structure that permits construction of transition matrices for each country. In all three countries, the sample is restricted to individuals aged 15–65. The industries are aggregated into five sectors: agriculture, mining, construction, and utilities; manufacturing; commerce, hotels, and restaurants; and other services. Each subsector is then subdivided between formal and informal workers. A worker who is eligible for social security benefits is considered formal. There is a residual sector that captures individuals who are either unemployed or out of the labor force.

The *Encuesta Nacional de Ocupación y Empleo* (National Occupation and Employment Survey, ENOE) is used to calculate transition matrices for Mexico. The ENOE is a household survey that collects detailed information on labor force status, wages, and occupational and demographic characteristics. It has been collected quarterly since 2005 and is representative both nationally and by state. The sample size is about 120,260 households each quarter. Each household is interviewed in five consecutive quarters; during each quarter, one-fifth of the sample is replaced. The transition matrix is constructed by looking at the first and fifth interview. Six year-to-year transition matrices are derived, the first reflecting transitions between 2005 and 2006 and the most recent transitions between 2010 and 2011.

The Morocco Labor Force Survey is nationally representative and covers both rural and urban areas. The survey is collected quarterly and the rotating panel consists of two interviews for each household one year apart. For example, households interviewed in the first quarter of 2006 were interviewed again in the first quarter of 2007. Year-to-year transition matrices cover 2006–11 (see Verme et al. 2014).

The *Pesquisa Mensal de Emprego* is the Brazilian Labor Force Survey. The survey collects detailed information on Brazil's labor market but is representative only of six metropolitan (urban) regions. Each wave of the survey samples about 120,000 individuals. Each household is interviewed 12 times over an 18-month period. In each wave of the survey, individuals are identified in their first interview and followed a year later at the time of their fifth interview. Like the other two countries, four year-to-year matrices are derived that cover 2007–11.

Administrative data from social security records are used in chapter 4 for Morocco and Costa Rica. This information provides an immensely rich source of data to estimate heterogeneous labor mobility costs across industries, as well as workers of different formality status and firm sizes. In Costa Rica, social security records provide monthly wage and employment data at the four digit ISIC level from January 2006 through March 2011. Workers with two or more jobs, less than 12 monthly observations, or low monthly wages are dropped from the sample. On average, each quarter the sample consists of 866,415 workers. In Morocco, social security records are available for 2006, 2008, and 2010. The sample averages 81,288 workers a year.

Reduced-Form Analysis of the Impact of Structural Reform on Labor Outcomes

The macro-level regression analysis in chapter 5 based on Hollweg, Lederman, and Mitra (2012) used data on the dates of structural reforms and the country sample from Wacziarg and Welch (2008), which proxies for the year when countries reached a threshold of broad economic reform, such as macroeconomic stabilization, privation, trade opening, and the end of interventionist states, such as communism. The sample consists of 88 countries, the majority being developing countries since most developed countries had already reformed during the sample period.

Six labor market outcomes are considered separately as dependent variables of interest. The unemployment rate is defined as the percentage of the labor force that is without work but available for and seeking employment. The series was constructed using data from the International Monetary Fund *International Financial Statistics* (IFS), the World Bank *World Development Indicators* (WDI), and the International Labour Organization (ILO) *Key Indicators of the Labour Market*, the OECD *Labor Force Statistics*, and other regional agency and country-specific sources. Employment measured in millions is accessed from the Conference Board *Total Economy Database* (TED), and includes employees, the self-employed, unpaid family members who are economically engaged, apprentices, and the military. Employment series for countries not available from the TED were accessed from the WDI as total workers aged 15 and older. Female employment measured in millions is accessed from the WDI and represents women workers aged 15 and older. The wage index, accessed from the IFS, is an index of wage earnings with 2005 equal to 100 as the base year.

The labor force participation rate, accessed from the WDI, is the labor force as a percentage of the working-age population. Total labor force comprises people ages 15 and older who meet the ILO definition of the economically active population: all people who supply labor for the production of goods and services during a specified period. It includes both employed and unemployed. While national practices vary in the treatment of groups such as the armed forces and seasonal or part-time workers, in general the labor force includes the armed forces, the unemployed, and first-time job seekers but excludes homemakers and other unpaid caregivers and informal workers. Labor force participation rate series for countries not available from the WDI were accessed from the IFS as the labor force as a percentage of the population aged 15 and older. The female labor force participation rate, accessed from the WDI, is women workers as a percentage of the female working-age population.

Reduced-Form Analysis of the Impact of Displacement on Labor Outcomes

For the micro-level regressions on the impact of displacement on employment and wage outcomes after a trade-related shock, based on Arias-Vázquez and Lederman (2013), data come from the household-level Mexican Labor Force

Survey (*Encuesta Nacional de Ocupacion y Empleo*). This survey collects detailed information on labor force status, wages, employment, and demographic characteristics of the labor force. The survey has been collected quarterly since 2005 and covers about 120,000 households. Arias-Vázquez and Lederman (2013) restrict the sample to individuals aged 15–65. Selected phases of the survey were used that implemented an extended questionnaire (2005: Q1–Q4; 2006: Q1–Q2; 2007: Q2; 2008: Q2; 2009: Q1; and 2001: Q1), which collected detailed information on individual labor histories. The survey asks whether individuals have ever experienced a job separation that left them temporarily unemployed, and if yes, to state the reason for it. The resulting sample covers 786,800 individuals.

References

Arias-Vázquez, F. J., E. Artuç, D. Lederman, and D. Rojas. 2013. "Trade, Informal Employment and Labor Adjustment Costs." Policy Research Working Paper 6614, World Bank, Washington, DC.

Arias-Vázquez, F. J., and D. Lederman. 2013. "Displaced Workers and Labor Market Outcomes: Evidence from Mexico." Unpublished manuscript, International Trade Department, Poverty Reduction and Economic Management, World Bank, Washington, DC.

Artuç, E., S. Chaudhuri, and J. McLaren. 2008. "Delay and Dynamics in Labor Market Adjustment: Simulation Results." *Journal of International Economics* 75 (1): 1–13.

Artuç, E., D. Lederman, and G. Porto. 2013. "A Mapping of Labor Mobility Costs in the Developing World." Policy Research Working Paper 6556, World Bank, Washington, DC.

Hollweg, C. H., D. Lederman, and D. Mitra. 2012. "Structural Reforms and Labor-Market Outcomes: International Panel Data Evidence." Unpublished manuscript, International Trade Department, Poverty Reduction and Economic Management, World Bank, Washington, DC.

Kaplan, D. S., D. Lederman, and R. Robertson. 2013. "Worker-Level Adjustment Costs in a Developing Country: Evidence from Mexico." Unpublished manuscript, International Trade Department, Poverty Reduction and Economic Management, World Bank, Washington, DC.

Verme, P., A. G. Barry, J. Guennouni, and M. Taamouti. 2014. "Labor Mobility, Economic Shocks, and Jobless Growth." Policy Research Working Paper 6795, World Bank, Washington, DC.

Wacziarg, R., and K. H. Welch. 2008. "Trade Liberalization and Growth: New Evidence." *World Bank Economic Review* 22 (2): 187–231.

Mapping Labor Mobility and Labor Adjustment Costs and Gains from Trade

		Gains from trade		Labor adjustment costs		
	Mobililty costs (C)	Potential	Actual	% of initial welfare	% of potential gain	% of actual gain
Peru	7.94	4.32	−2.93	7.25	1.68	2.47
Azerbaijan	7.81	19.58	13.79	5.79	0.30	0.42
Turkey	7.39	6.45	0.53	5.92	0.92	11.17
Ethiopia	7.06	8.46	5.44	3.02	0.36	0.56
Bangladesh	6.55	15.04	11.14	3.90	0.26	0.35
Indonesia	6.20	13.15	9.15	4.00	0.30	0.44
Lithuania	6.07	8.19	3.01	5.18	0.63	1.72
Chile	5.72	3.62	0.58	3.04	0.84	5.24
Ecuador	5.53	4.83	2.39	2.45	0.51	1.03
Bulgaria	5.47	6.02	3.05	2.97	0.49	0.97
France	5.33	3.40	0.79	2.61	0.77	3.30
Denmark	5.08	2.26	-0.28	2.54	1.12	9.07
Egypt, Arab Rep.	4.95	7.47	5.64	1.82	0.24	0.32
Bolivia	4.93	5.44	4.00	1.44	0.26	0.36
Mongolia	4.88	5.71	4.40	1.31	0.23	0.30
Russian Federation	4.56	8.94	7.20	1.74	0.19	0.24
Iran, Islamic Rep.	4.52	5.81	4.71	1.09	0.19	0.23
Georgia	4.42	5.52	4.59	0.93	0.17	0.20
Syrian Arab Republic	4.40	8.93	7.58	1.35	0.15	0.18
India	4.35	8.45	7.76	0.69	0.08	0.09
Mauritania	4.33	18.43	16.63	1.81	0.10	0.11
Jordan	4.13	6.32	5.46	0.87	0.14	0.16
Oman	4.01	5.04	4.21	0.83	0.16	0.20
Senegal	3.68	4.52	4.24	0.28	0.06	0.07
Poland	2.99	4.57	4.15	0.43	0.09	0.10

table continues next page

Appendix C *(continued)*

		Gains from trade		Labor adjustment costs		
	Mobility costs (C)	Potential	Actual	% of initial welfare	% of potential gain	% of actual gain
Czech Republic	2.97	4.61	4.18	0.43	0.09	0.10
Greece	2.72	2.02	1.80	0.22	0.11	0.12
Belgium	2.57	2.01	1.83	0.18	0.09	0.10
Costa Rica	2.56	2.26	2.03	0.23	0.10	0.11
Austria	2.46	1.69	1.55	0.15	0.09	0.10
Romania	2.40	4.76	4.55	0.21	0.04	0.05
Portugal	2.17	2.47	2.29	0.17	0.07	0.07
Germany	2.16	1.72	1.65	0.07	0.04	0.04
Canada	2.13	1.31	1.19	0.13	0.10	0.11
Sweden	2.04	1.79	1.67	0.12	0.07	0.07
Finland	2.00	1.89	1.77	0.12	0.06	0.07
South Africa	1.95	2.52	2.43	0.09	0.04	0.04
Slovak Republic	1.91	2.70	2.58	0.12	0.04	0.05
Norway	1.88	1.45	1.36	0.09	0.06	0.07
Spain	1.86	1.54	1.45	0.09	0.06	0.06
Ireland	1.81	0.57	0.45	0.13	0.23	0.29
United Kingdom	1.75	1.02	0.93	0.09	0.09	0.10
Korea, Rep.	1.57	1.78	1.70	0.08	0.04	0.05
Latvia	1.55	2.18	2.07	0.11	0.05	0.05
Japan	1.42	1.64	1.58	0.06	0.04	0.04
United States	1.16	0.55	0.50	0.06	0.11	0.12
Singapore	1.09	0.78	0.71	0.07	0.09	0.10

Source: Artuç, Lederman, and Porto 2013.
Note: The first column presents estimated aggregate labor mobility cost for each country expressed as a ratio of the annual average real wage. The potential gains from trade measure the percentage gains in welfare of a worker in the food and beverage sector after a 30 percent price decline in the sector due to trade liberalization but in the absence of mobility costs. The actual gains from trade measure the percentage gains in welfare when there are mobility costs. Potential and actual welfare gains are for workers in the food and beverage sector and therefore represent a lower bound of the welfare gains economy-wide. Labor adjustment costs, the difference between the potential and actual gains from trade, are expressed as a percent of initial welfare. The last two columns express labor adjustment costs as a ratio of potential and actual gains from trade.

Reference

Artuç, E., D. Lederman, and G. Porto. 2013. "A Mapping of Labor Mobility Costs in the Developing World." Policy Research Working Paper 6556, World Bank, Washington, DC.

Environmental Benefits Statement

The World Bank Group is committed to reducing its environmental footprint. In support of this commitment, the Publishing and Knowledge Division leverages electronic publishing options and print-on-demand technology, which is located in regional hubs worldwide. Together, these initiatives enable print runs to be lowered and shipping distances decreased, resulting in reduced paper consumption, chemical use, greenhouse gas emissions, and waste.

The Publishing and Knowledge Division follows the recommended standards for paper use set by the Green Press Initiative. Whenever possible, books are printed on 50 percent to 100 percent postconsumer recycled paper, and at least 50 percent of the fiber in our book paper is either unbleached or bleached using Totally Chlorine Free (TCF), Processed Chlorine Free (PCF), or Enhanced Elemental Chlorine Free (EECF) processes.

More information about the Bank's environmental philosophy can be found at http://crinfo.worldbank.org/wbcrinfo/node/4.

green press INITIATIVE

www.ingramcontent.com/pod-product-compliance
Lightning Source LLC
Chambersburg PA
CBHW082359270326
41935CB00013B/1689